GW00702143

TABLE OF CONTENTS

ACKNOWLEDGMENTS

I would like to acknowledge several people, beginning with my parents, Henry and Joan Parkinson, and brothers Dan and Ken Parkinson. They have always supported me and my ambitions. I would not be the man I am today without them.

I would like to thank my wife, Michelle Parkinson, and my beautiful girls, Alyssa and Miranda. Your support and understanding is appreciated.

This book would not be possible without the support of Nancy Hunter Denney. She challenged me to stay on task. You are an amazing woman and I truly appreciate your assistance.

A special thanks to Rich Hurley from Bryant University for inspiring me with new ideas and concepts—keep up the great work! In addition, Rebecca Lindley from Fitchburg State University has been a great supporter. Your creative writing skills were a tremendous help. Furthermore, I would like to thank Jamie Cochran, Scott Lyons, and Meagan Sage for your peer reviews. Your feedback was greatly appreciated.

Finally, I would like to thank and acknowledge all the faculty, staff, and students from Bryant University and Fitchburg State University who helped shape the Parkinson's Leadership Development Program.

ENDORSEMENT

There is growing challenge confronting college campuses. It's the development of the nations leaders for the future. Employers are telling us that they want to see leadership development on the resumes of their applicants, and they expect that process to begin by age twenty-one. *Creating a Leadership Program One Stage at a Time* squarely addresses that need. It is a highly accessible, extremely practical, and thoroughly comprehensive primer on the vital concepts in leadership and leadership development in use today on college campuses. Henry Parkinson asks the tough questions and then provides meaningful guidance to all those whose job is to create student leadership programs. In sharing designs of his and other leadership programs, he models the kind of servant leadership he writes about. This book is a terrific place to begin creating your leadership development programs for your students.

Jim Kouzes

Coauthor of *The Leadership Challenge*, and the Dean's Executive Fellow of Leadership, Leavey School of Business, Santa Clara University

FORWARD

On my desk is a simple paperweight with the following words: "What would you attempt to do if you knew you could not fail?" I can't recall when I received this paperweight, but I know it was a gift. I can't remember when I first put it on my desk, but now it serves as an anchor. In fact, no matter how many piles I have cluttering my workspace; somehow, I make sure that I can always see this quote.

This quote holds power and meaning for me on many levels. Most importantly, in this context, it reminds me of the incredible gift leadership educators, and anyone working with young people, can offer. We can offer these words directly or indirectly to others. We can challenge and support them to answer this question throughout their leadership journey. In over twenty years of working with young people, these words underpin a basic philosophy of leadership development that I hold. Simply put, leadership is available to all of us; the question is: are you ready to step in, make the choice to lead, and give it all you have?

Henry Parkinson has given us a rich resource to support our work in leadership education, training, and development. In this text, you'll benefit from his research and years of practice in the field of student leadership development. The gifts he gives the reader are many - a useful summary of a large body of theory and models of leadership; a simple but not simplistic model that bridges theory and practice in the Parkinson's Leadership Development Program (PLDP); and a powerful assessment tool. And all of this is both easily accessible and applicable for the busy campus-based leadership educator.

Over the years, I've worked with many campus-based leadership development educators. They work in student activities, residence life, orientation, service learning, athletics, academic affairs… the list goes on. One of the few commonalities I've discovered is that no one has enough time to do all the work they want to with their students. The beauty of the PLDP is that it gives you the gift of time. Here you have an approach and a strategy to adapt and implement for your campus and your students. You don't have to create something from nothing. The PLDP gives you everything you need to develop a powerful leadership development program. Additionally, the PLDP suggests a model for those of us working with and for students. You will grow and develop as you bring this work forward for your students and your campus.

I encourage you to take time with this book. Read it and use it. It's as much a guidebook as it is a text. In this text, you will find more than you might need, and that's why it's like a guidebook. Keep this book handy. Down the road, I'm going to guess you'll come back to it because of the great breadth of content shared.

So…what would *you* attempt to do if you knew you could not fail? I say take the first step by reading this book and challenging yourself to not just think "what's next?" but to start down that road and take the first step. Your students will be grateful.

Marcy Levy Shankman, Ph.D.

Co-author, *Emotionally Intelligent Leadership: A Guide For College Students*

PREFACE

You may find all you need to know in one chart, chapter or quote. You may find new ideas on how to offer more programs for less money or a new strategy on how to better sequence your course content. You may also come to realize that minor adjustments to your current efforts may have a major impact. This is an introduction to creating a comprehensive leadership program on your campus. Your efforts cannot start and end here. If you are committed to this challenge, you will have do additional research, but the hope is that this book gives you a head start on this journey.

Like an artist staring at a blank canvas, the leadership educator struggles to determine the best mediums, colors, and brush strokes to create a masterful outcome. Common questions include: Where do I begin? What matters most given my limited resources? How does the order of what I offer impact potential learning outcomes? And, what role should my personal leadership competencies and interests play in my planning process?

These are important questions to answer to ensure the best use of your time and talents. After all, you can be skilled at organization, but not know what you are trying to plan. You can be well versed in The Social Change Model, yet not have the teaching abilities or methodologies to engage students and foster their enthusiasm about the subject matter. You can also have wonderful and diversified programming ideas, but lack a cohesive plan of attack for a logical developmental progression of leadership aptitudes, understandings and inspirations. It's also possible you were never trained as a leadership practitioner and now you find yourself seeking ways to carry out ever changing (albeit exciting) job responsibilities. Consequently, the question must be raised, "Is there a right and wrong way to build your leadership program?"

Unlike the painter whose talent is judged by those who become personally involved with the colors, images and self-identified meaning of the artist's work, the leadership educator is accountable to a host of evaluative measures including: industries best practices, historical data, mission statements, professional standards, current research and assessment criteria – to name a few. The "success" or "proficiency" of your efforts should not consist of subjective interpretations like whether or not your students "felt like they have a better understanding of leadership," "found the material helpful," or "would highly recommend your leadership class to their peers." Your goal is to be intentional, responsible and accountable in planning of your leadership programming.

By combining the findings of doctoral research on student leadership development with years of experience training leaders, this book outlines the bridge between theory and practice. The result is a book designed to assist the student affairs practitioner with the planning, implementation, delivery, and evaluation of leadership development programs targeted towards college students.

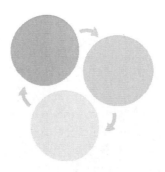

CHAPTER 1

The Importance of Developing Leaders

Introduction

A blank screen stares back at you, daring the impossible. You begin typing only to hold down the "delete" key moments later. Silently you think to yourself, "this should be easy!" You have plenty of great ideas and sufficient resources to create a "plan of attack" for offering leadership development opportunities to a diverse range of students. So, what's the problem? Your fingers remain still. Is it possible you have too many paths you could pursue? Is it possible you don't know which one leads to the greatest reward?

Your eyes move to the stack of books at your feet. On the very top is *The Seven Habits of Highly Effective People* by Dr. Stephen Covey. You quickly scan the row of spines beneath and note another familiar cover, *How to Win Friends and Influence Others* by Dale Carnegie. Although dated in some ways, you appreciate how both are timeless, essential reads. There are some leadership books recommended by friends, and those you picked up at conferences. Your stack also contains "must haves" like *The Leadership Challenge* by James Kouzes and Dr. Barry Posner, along with *Exploring*

Leadership: College Students Who Want to Make a Difference by Drs. Susan Komives, Nance Lucas, and Timothy Mc-Mahon. Also on your stack are the latest theoretical top sellers that you read about on the NCLP list-serve. You look towards the bottom of the stack, and there are books you are dying to read when you get the chance, like *The Four Agreements* by Don Miguel Ruiz, *Good to Great* by Jim Collins, *First Break All the Rules* by Marcus Buckingham, and *Leadership* and *The One Minute Manager* by Dr. Ken Blanchard.

But perhaps the above description does not fit you at all. Instead, glancing away from your computer screen and looking around your office, you see nothing but floor at your feet—no stacks of books, magazines, articles, or binders. You literally have nothing. It becomes clear: you don't know what it is you don't know. There's enough on your plate and the very thought of creating "one more thing" or "doing more with less" is exhausting. You think to yourself, "Why am I making this so difficult?" There has to be some program on another campus that you can replicate.

Whatever your situation, failing to optimize the quality of your leadership offerings comes at a significant cost to those you serve and hinders your professional development and personal satisfaction. Your students will either be positively influenced *or not* by your efforts, so you don't have the latitude to be "average" or "beige" in your leadership offerings. Failure is not an option in the competitive environment of higher education. You train your students to be less than exceptional when you bring your "C" game.

The Value and Purpose of Leadership Development

Leadership educators, student activities professionals, and anyone else involved in the training of students has the potential to influence the quality of leaders entering society. The world needs strong leaders who are civically engaged, seek social justice, and possess both theoretical knowledge and the practical skills necessary to implement it. From the founding fathers of higher education to contemporary researchers, the imperative is clear: for the betterment of society we must prepare students.

In 1995, in an article entitled *In Leadership Studies: A New Partnership Between Academic Departments and Student Affairs,* John Burns, an assistant professor in the Department of Educational Leadership and Counseling Psychology at Washington State University wrote that, "producing such leaders for society has been the traditional role of higher education", (p. 242). And in an article entitled *Leading the Way: Colleges Recognize Growing Need to Offer Leadership Programs,* Suzanne Brach points out that, "the increasing interest in leadership is related to national interest in civic education, character development and support for young people developing values and vision in their lives" (p. 5). Your efforts will prepare the future leaders of our schools, government, work force, spiritual and religious communities, and volunteer agencies. Your efforts will also assist students of all ages to become positive role models and contributing citizens.

Kirk Buckner and Lee Williams (1995), in *Re-Conceptualizing University Student Leadership Development Programs: Applying the Completing Values Model,* state that one of the central purposes of student leadership development programs is to "provide a comprehensive offering of activities and services to complement an academic education" (p.1). With the growing complexities of society and the need for students to cope with constant change, leadership programs are indispensable. They support the educational mission of a university by taking theoretical concepts and providing opportunities for students to apply in practice what they've learned in theory. Leadership expert and researcher Sara Boatman points out in *The Leadership Audit: A Process to Enhance the Development of Student Leadership,* 1999, that nearly every college and university has an expressed commitment to the development of students as leaders. "Helping students develop the integrity and strength of character that prepare them for leadership may be one of the most challenging and important goals of higher education" (cited in Dugan

& Komives, 2007, p. 8).

The logical progression of the increased attention on leadership education is further supported by leadership research experts Christine Cress, Helen Astin, Kathleen Zimmerman-Oster, and John Burkhardt. In their 2001 article, *Developmental Outcomes of College Students' Involvement in Leadership Activities, Journal for College Student Development*, the authors concluded, "the amount of student learning and personal development is directly proportional to the quality and quantity of student involvement in the process of learning, including participation in leadership experiences and activities" (p. 16). The results of this study clearly highlighted that participants were more likely to grow to develop their sense of civic responsibility, become more skilled at conflict resolution, planning and implementing activities, and be more willing to take risks compared to those students who did not participate in leadership programming. To further support the importance of the work of leadership educators, Dugan and Komives point out in *Developing Leadership Capacity in College Students: Findings for a National Study* that "students can and do increase their leadership skills during the college years and that increases in leadership development in turn enhance the self-efficacy, civic engagement, character development, academic performance, and personal development of students" (2007, p. 8).

One of the more practical justifications for your leadership programming efforts, however, doesn't have anything to do with what some have labeled the "soft" outcomes of higher education (as mentioned above). It's financial! There is value to the institution from a marketing perspective or "cost-benefit" analysis. Students with significant leadership training and advanced leadership skills, including train-ability and demonstrated abilities to work collaboratively, are desirable candidates in the marketplace. They get hired and ensure employer confidence that graduates can work well in teams and adapt to change. So, there is not only personal, societal, and preparatory value in your programming efforts, there is a marketing and thus, financial benefit to be gained as well.

Staying Current

There are many common sense arguments for leadership programming that continue to be validated by research. Check out *Leadership: Current Theories, Research, and Future Directions* by Bruce Avolio, Fred Walumbwa, and Todd Weber (2009) or explore *Authentic Leadership: Rediscovering the Secrets to Creating Lasting Value* by Bill George (2003). Other resources that you might consider adding to your library include: *The Handbook for Student Leadership Development* by Susan Komives, John Dugan, Julie Owen, Craig Slack, and Wendy Wagner (2011), *Developing Students' Leadership Capacity* produced by *New Directions for Student Services* (2012), and *The Student Leadership Competences Guidebook* by Corey Seemiller (2014).

Finally, look for the article titled *Developing Leadership Capacity in College Students: Findings from a National Study* written by John Dugan and Susan Komives (2007).

New trends also bring new challenges. Dugan and Komives (2007) point out three overarching problems that practitioners should consider when developing their program:

- "A significant gap between theory and practice

- An unclear picture of the leadership development needs of college students

- Uncertainty regarding the influence of the college environment on leadership development outcomes" (p. 8)

There is a lot to consider! That is what makes this so complex. Leadership development is constantly evolving. It is up to us to keep up with the new trends, theories, frameworks, and models. That is why it is important that you start building your leadership library with the suggested resources in this book and beyond!

CHAPTER 2

Criteria for Effective Leadership Development Programs

The more things change, the more they remain the same. Although job titles and departmental names may have changed over the past three decades, there's no denying the prevalence of leadership education, like any other campus functional area, to support the overall mission of the college or university. Before ever adapting job titles (see below), those working to support the academic side of the house in earlier decades were simply called things like "director of student activities," "dean of student life," or "coordinator of student programming." Professional identity was more of a broad stroke of color across campus, sweeping from one side of the canvas to the other.

Today, the student activities professional's role in supporting the educational mission hasn't changed. All of us are still viewed as educators. Our identity is part of the entire college or university; not the "co-curricular" as much as an essential part of the overall academic curriculum itself. This is a good thing. Job titles have changed to better reflect the work that is given to us! As the "director of leadership and community service" or "coordinator of student engagement" or "assistant dean for student involvement and programming," your position most likely involves the training of student leaders. As such you are required to plan and implement "leadership development opportunities" for the entire community (including specific training for a diversity of organizations). Perhaps you teach a first year experience or leadership course, or are expected to be the leadership expert on your campus. One may also find themselves less involved in the day-to-day leadership program planning, but oversee this functional area. In any case, it is important to understand the big picture.

Ask the Tough Questions

What is a *leadership development opportunity*? Some believe it is the formal and informal means by which your efforts result in the advancement of understanding at the practical and theoretical levels, whereby students are inspired and prepared to be contributing members of their immediate community and society at large. Regardless of your title, you are a leadership educator! You lead by example, role model effective skills, design and teach a leadership course, select inspirational quotes to hang in key locations around campus, host a leadership conference, plan a weekend retreat and so on. One size doesn't fit all and it takes many different approaches to adequately meet the developmental needs of your students. Regardless of *how* you choose to proceed, give consideration to the "rules" or "criteria" from *which* to proceed!

Below is a list of nine essential questions to ask yourself and other campus partners, as you begin to plan or review where to exert your energy.

Does your program support the mission of the university?

One of the most important criteria for developing a leadership program is to align your efforts with the formal mission or purpose of your institution. A mission or purpose statement is a concise, intentional and revealing declaration of the goal of the school for its students. By aligning your leadership program with your institution's mission, you are making a direct connection to how your program(s) can and will add value to the work of the school as a whole. This is essential given the rising costs of higher education and subsequent reviews by accrediting agencies' decisions on decision-making and allocation of resources. How can you prove that you support a larger purpose or vision?

Does your program create a sense of civic responsibility within the university and in the surrounding community?

Preparing your students for life after college requires facilitating their engagement with their immediate surroundings. Whether in a programming board, governing council, residence hall community, or classroom setting, providing opportunities for the development of leadership skills, approaches, and attitudes which result in responsible citizens is relevant and essential. How can you encourage personal accountability, civil lines of communication, commitment to a collective living and learning environment, protecting the basic human rights of others, and actualizing equal access and inclusion?

Are your programs inclusive of all students regardless of their race, religion, national origin, gender identity, physical ability, or sexual orientation?

Based on the notion that students often learn what they live, when creating your leadership program it is important you include not only students with diverse interests, opinions, backgrounds, and majors, but remain sensitive to the various cultural, political, social, and religious characteristics of a modern society. Be open to ideas incorporating such appreciation and sensitivity to differences in your overall program efforts. One way to ensure inclusion is to take advantage of the wealth of diversity in your student population and faculty and engage them in the discussion through focus groups and one-on-one conversations. How can your programs demonstrate a commitment to being inclusive? For example, you may have a blind student participate in one of your programs; in that case, be sure that everything that is distributed is converted to braille.

Is your program supported by a trustworthy foundation to facilitate character development and societal change?

The popularity of leadership programming makes it easier to identify responsible definitions of leadership, models, and theories to incorporate into your programming efforts. Be honest with yourself: you don't always have the time, expertise, or resources to apply some of the more popular models. But often these models can be adapted and used as the foundation for a series of workshops, courses, or conferences.

Does your program utilize a progressive building approach to best meet the readiness and developmental needs of your students?

Freshmen usually do what they are instructed the first few weeks before realizing they need to start standing on their own two feet. Student leaders are motivated to learn about topics of leadership directly relevant to their personal lives before they are genuinely interested in learning how to make the world a better place. In other words, a natural progression of training is from the "me" to the "we." This "building block" approach not only applies to the sequencing of your efforts (for example, going from personal development, to group development and collaboration, to societal change), but also to the progression from individual skills to interpersonal skills. For example, emerging leaders require the basics (i.e. self-motivation) before they can appreciate the higher level skills (i.e. strategizing for social justice).

Does your program utilize a diversity of engagement strategies and multiple delivery methods?

Given the likelihood that your students spend hours

in classes taught in the traditional lecture style format, incorporating a diversity of experiential learning techniques, formats, and training methodologies will lead to increased engagement and interest. You have no choice but to make your entire approach creative and fun. Content is not lost. In fact, you will accomplish more of your learning outcomes when you expand the way you interact with your student learners. This becomes part of your planning process.

Does your program incorporate self-assessments and personal or group reflection?

Look in the mirror! How would you describe your reflection? This is a challenging question for professionals and almost impossible for your students to answer. Whether its ego, low self-esteem, immaturity, transition, or built-in defense mechanisms, many factors prevent them from even looking in the mirror. They need to learn how to self-assess and accept feedback from others. These skills will be developed when opportunities to practice self-assessment and reflection are present. How can you build someone's confidence and encourage them to honestly examine who they are and where they want to go?

Is your program set up to constantly assess and improve program effectiveness?

Leadership development is a continual process, therefore leadership education initiatives and programs should be responsive to the latest trends, newest research, and most current approaches. How do you know if your programs are contemporary and guided by legitimate work? By conducting the necessary assessments and comprehension checks, you will be able to determine if you are meeting your learning objectives and successfully developing student leaders.

Does your program have support at all levels?

You don't want to go too deep without institutional support for your leadership program. This is not limited to financial support, but includes staffing and administrative support as well. Also, consider how you will sustain your program given your other responsibilities. When trying to solicit support, it's helpful to provide research, learning objectives, case studies, and examples of other institutions with successful programs.

Finding an academic home for your leadership program is a much tougher sell than acquiring buy-in from student affairs' administrators. It is recommended that you involve faculty in the early stages of your planning and, if possible, work to establish leadership certificate programs or an academic minor in leadership.

Unfortunately, many institutions lack the resources to fully support a comprehensive leadership development program or minor, and very few have separate offices that coordinate leadership development initiatives. Though interns and graduate assistants can be valuable contributors to the planning and implementation of leadership programming, it is hard to sustain a leadership program without having a professional staff member to take the lead.

And, last of all, don't forget students! In addition to faculty and administration, student involvement in program development discussions is vital to their ultimate buy-in. Many students are highly capable of planning and implementing programs, setting up speakers, designing training sessions, and handling many of the details involved in hosting a leadership conference. Student involvement in the process provides an opportunity for advanced leaders (those who have exhibited a high level of leadership skills) to apply their skills to practice and give back to the program.

Before getting too far along in the process, stop and see if what you are doing meets the criteria above. Start small and build from there. It will take time to convince those with a "show me" mentality. Always try to do something rather than doing nothing. As previously noted, you are the educator. If you don't offer any leadership development programming, they get what they get—nothing. Is that good enough?

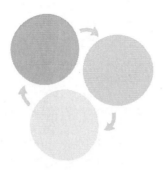

CHAPTER 3

Google It: Definitions of Leadership

What is "leadership"? Your answer to this question can't help but influence how you teach. If you were to type "definitions of leadership" in your Google search function, you would find over 36 million potential resources. The very discussion of leadership raises exciting questions:

- Are leaders born?

- Is leadership earned or learned?

- What is the immediate or ultimate goal of leadership?

- How do followers' responses determine the leader's effectiveness?

- What does the definition say about the era?

- How do other areas of development interface with a leader's potential?

- How is leading different than managing?

- What characteristics make for an effective leader?

The more these questions can be answered by one concise definition, the easier it will be for you to develop leadership programming. A collection of definitions is offered on the following pages.

Definitions of Leaders and Leadership

As you read the list of additional definitions below, consider how each definition is consistent with your ideals and vision. Which offers a solid foundation for your diverse educational efforts and needs? Which will be useful in building a single training workshop, certificate program, course, visual or promotional campaign, retreat or lecture series? Which will help direct your leadership development programming?

Leadership is ultimately about change, and…effective leaders are those who are able to effect positive change on behalf of others and society.

-Amirianzadeh, Jaafari, Ghourchian, and Jowkar in *College Student Leadership Competencies Development: A Model*

Leadership is an activity or set of activities, observable to others, that occurs in a group, organization, or institution and which involves a leader and followers who willingly subscribe to common purposes and work together to achieve them.

- Kenneth and Miriam Clark in *Choosing to Lead*

Leadership is a process which means that it is not a trait or characteristic that resides in the leader, but is a transactional event that occurs between the leader and his or her followers.

- Peter Northouse in *Leadership Theory and Practice*

Leadership is the art of mobilizing others to want to struggle for shared aspirations.

- James Kouzes and Barry Posner in *The Leadership Challenge*

A genuine leader is not a searcher for consensus but a molder of consensus.

-Martin Luther King, Jr.

A leader is a dealer in hope.

-Napoleon Bonaparte

My definition of a leader ... is a man who can persuade people to do what they don't want to do, or do what they're too lazy to do, and like it.

-Harry S. Truman, 1884-1972, Thirty-third President of the United States

The leader can never close the gap between himself and the group. If he does, he is no longer what he must be. He must walk a tightrope between the consent he must win and the control he must exert.

-Vince Lombardi

People ask the difference between a leader and a boss. The leader leads, and the boss drives.

-Theodore Roosevelt

A leader is best when people barely know he exists, when his work is done, his aim fulfilled, they will say: we did it ourselves.

-Lao Tzu

The only definition of a leader is someone who has followers.

-Peter Drucker

Leadership is a function of knowing yourself, having a vision that is well communicated, building trust among colleagues, and taking effective action to realize your own leadership potential.

-Warren Bennis

Making the Connection

Given your life and professional experience, which of the above definitions resonated with you? How does the definition you choose fit into the mission of your institution? It's important to be personally connected to what you are creating so that you maintain the level of passion needed to be authentic and truly committed to the success of your program. However, it is equally important to make sure that your work is in line with the mission of your institution. Find a balance!

Too often, professionals get caught up in what "everyone else is doing" or feel obligated to go down a certain path, when in truth you don't agree or find the content engaging! This applies not only to the definition of leadership you select, but to the selection of a theory or model of leadership. If you don't understand it, neither will your students!

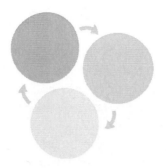

CHAPTER 4

Starting with the End in Mind: Learning Outcomes

Have you heard the saying, "Start with the end in mind?" Knowing where you are trying to take your students developmentally will help determine how you get them there. How will they be different because of your leadership development programming? Before you start looking at specific activities, room availability, or scheduling, think about the big picture. Start by taking out a blank sheet of paper and asking a very simple question, "As a result of participating in Program X or Course Y, how will my students have changed?"

Writing your learning outcomes does not require a lot of time, and does not have to contain fancy words you can't pronounce. Learning outcomes are intended to guide and direct your efforts while establishing the criteria to evaluate effectiveness. Well written learning outcomes give you the structure to best identify the methods you should use to communicate the content and skills.

Learning outcomes should be intentional and as specific as possible, forcing you to hone in on what matters most.

Driving Your Content

Not only does this process help you to narrow down the scope of your content, it forces you to consider how that content will be delivered. For example, if you are teaching collaboration strategies, does it make more sense to use small-group discussions or a lecture format? In small groups, students could be asked to define the term "collaboration." You can then ask the groups to identify their process, any obstacles they had to overcome, and what strategies served them well. By doing so they are literally engaged in the art of collaboration. Though a lecture may play some part in the program, small-group discussions would be particularly effective, given your content. Being intentional connects *how* you deliver the content with *what* students learn from the exchange, thus maximizing the efficiency of your efforts.

As noted earlier, when it comes to learning outcomes, less is more! A few well thought-out learning outcomes can be used to organize your great ideas and goals into a manageable workshop, class, course, or series. Below are tips on writing learning outcomes.

Tips on Writing Learning Outcomes:

- In preparation for writing your outcomes, review your university's mission statement.

- Start with a blank screen and ask, "What do I want my students to know (content) and be able to do (skills) as a result of attending this program, event, workshop, or course?" In other words, you are asking the question, "How do I want my students to change, grow, learn and develop?"

- Review existing learning outcomes (Council for the Advancement of Standards).

- Perform a quick literature review of a particular topic and see what learning outcomes you can draw from your research.

- Consider items from the examples of learning outcomes provided below.

- Share your thoughts with colleagues, supervisors, and students to confirm you are on the right path.

- Be willing to let go of a few outcomes to avoid taking on more than is realistic.

Standard Desirable Outcomes

There are some learning outcomes that should be incorporated into every educational and training experience. Your programming efforts, for instance, should always include the intention to build the participant's level of self-confidence and self-esteem. Central to the achievement and appreciation of all other outcomes is whether or not participants feel worthy of improving, learning, and change. Are they in a place where they can even hear what you are attempting to teach them?

In the absence of a positive sense of self, you can still offer information and appeal to a student's intellectual development. However, leadership development requires the ability to connect what's being taught to personal experience and potential growth. Therefore, students must be able to sense the relevancy of your content to their own lives without insecurity, denial, or other self-defenses. Building confidence comes before students are capable of learning and appreciating: self-assessment, conflict resolution, self-management, healthy relationship building, goal setting, teamwork, and feedback.

Examples of Learning Outcomes

Below is an entire list of potential learning outcomes by category. Within each category you can choose a general statement to simply reflect that is an area that will be taught, or you can break down the learning within that area to be more specific. Go through this list a few times and check off a combination of general and specific outcomes.

Edit and revise the suggestions below to better fit your participants and programming needs.

Communication Skills:

- Students will be capable of identifying sources of conflict and work through them to resolution;

- Students will understand the process of communication;

- Students will be equipped with various skills of communication;

- Students will engage in assertive and constructive discussion, while avoiding quarreling;

- Students will be able to adapt a presentation to meet the needs of a particular audience.

Creativity:

- Students will be inspired to think out of the box;

- Students will understand the role of thinking differently as it assists the leader.

Curiosity:

- Students will take an active role in the learning process;

- Students will be encouraged to develop a greater interest in a variety of leadership topics;

- Students will learn research skills for acquiring new information and perspectives.

Delegation:

- Students will appreciate the empowerment value of delegation along with the basic skill set.

Diversity Appreciation and Sensitivity:

- Students will have an appreciation for the opinions of others;

- Students will explore the range of motivations behind behaviors;

- Students will appreciate the value in not judging others;

- Students will feel connected to diverse opinions;

- Students will challenge misplaced assumptions.

Giving and Taking Feedback:

- Students will give and accept feedback concerning personal development and leadership potential.

Goal Identification:

- Students will identify their personal goals and connect each goal to a specific leadership objective.

Knowing Oneself:

- Students will feel safe having difficult (or challenging) conversations;

- Students will be inspired to facilitate other's self-discovery by experiencing its positive effects;

- Student's inaccurate self-perceptions and leadership assumptions will be challenged consistently in a caring manner;

- Students will become more "trainable" and open to self-assessment and feedback;

- Students will seek a higher moral standard.

Motivation:

- Students will develop an enhanced sense of obligation to reach higher;

- Students will be encouraged and inspired to grow;

- Students will be inspired to seek additional information about leadership on their own;

- Students will learn how to apply motivation strategies;

- Students will develop a greater understanding of internal and external motivation;

- Students will take ownership of their decision making.

Problem Solving:

- Students will have developed skills for solving complex problems.

Self-Confidence:

- Students will experience a growth in confidence and self-esteem;

- Students will develop a deeper sense of self-worth.

Seek Knowledge:

- Students will learn the skill sets fundamental to leadership development;

- Students will engage in various forms of self-assessment;

- Students will desire more information about themselves and their goals.

Self-Management:

- Students will have the ability to change course or "let go" of unproductive traits and let others provide a new direction;

- Students will assume the ultimate ownership to maximize their leadership development potential;

Service to Others:

- Students will possess an enhanced sense of civic responsibility;

- Students will make a personal connection to contributing as a leader;

- Students will identify the relevancy of any leadership topic to their ability to positively influence the common good;

Team Work:

- Students will learn to collaborate across academic disciplines;

- Students will work collaboratively with the college community to serve the local community;

- Students will learn the art of relationship building;

- Students will feel an enhanced sense of connectedness and belonging to a group;

- Students will be proficient in establishing high performance teams;

- Students will understand and consider various group roles and obstacles to group performance;

- Students will be better able to negotiate towards a common mission or objective;

- Students will be able to identify group goals and set agendas to accomplish those goals;

- Students will value different perspectives;

In addition, the *Council for the Advancement of Standards in Higher Education (*Council for the Advancement of Standards, *2006)*, an extremely reliable source, has developed 13 learning outcomes to consider as you create your Student Leadership Programs.

Developing learning outcomes is a critical part of developing a comprehensive leadership development program. Outcomes provide direction and a strong foundation for your program. Learning outcomes will help identify the overall purpose of your leadership program, as well as organize your delivery approach. Finally, learning outcomes provide credibility for your work. If you can develop and measure learning outcomes, you can provide evidence to campus administrators that your program is successful and, in turn, allow you to gain additional resources for growing your program.

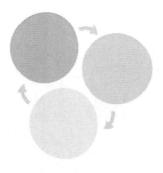

CHAPTER 5

Models, Frameworks, Theories

Before an artist begins to paint, he or she first reaches for a paintbrush. This is not a random selection, but the result of a craft developed over years of practice and familiarity with the process. As you begin the process of developing leaders through your leadership development and training efforts, what foundation (beyond a few definitions mentioned in the last chapter) will best serve your needs? Is there a particular model, theory, or framework that fits your institution and allows you to meet your learning outcomes? When reviewing the list of theories and frameworks in this chapter, ask yourself the following questions:

Do you understand it?

Does it resonate with you?

Does is excite you?

Can you wrap your head around it?

Can you build upon it and align theory with practice?

Does it flow for you?

Is it consistent with your leadership vision and beliefs?

Does it lend itself to your purposes by being flexible, adaptable, fluid and fun?

This chapter will describe many different resources that you can use when creating your leadership programs. It will include models and frameworks to guide your leadership programming. It will also include theories from experts in the field of leadership development who have researched the best practices for developing leaders. It is important to note that this chapter is only a taste of what could be adopted by your leadership program. The goal is to get you started, but it will be up to you to continue your research.

Models

Models give you a contextual guideline for your leadership development program. Look for a model or two that can serve as the backbone of your program. The first part of this chapter will explore three models for your consideration.

Social Change Model
© The Regents of The University of California

The *Social Change Model* of leadership development, which was developed by the Higher Education Research Institute (1996) at the University of California, Los Angeles, is one example of how students can become more civically responsible by participating in leadership development programs. The goals of this model are to enhance student learning and development and to increase self-knowledge and leadership competency. According to the Higher Education Research Institute, the model is inclusive in that it is designed to enhance the development of leadership qualities in all participants. Leadership is viewed as a process, rather than a position, and it promotes personal, group, and community values, social justice, self-knowledge, personal empowerment, collaboration, citizenship, and service.

The model breaks down leadership development into three focus areas: the individual, the group, and the com-

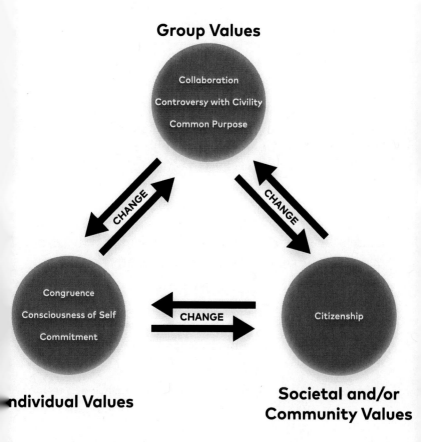

Group Values

Collaboration

Controversy with Civility

Common Purpose

CHANGE

CHANGE

CHANGE

Congruence

Consciousness of Self

Commitment

Citizenship

ndividual Values

**Societal and/or
Community Values**

munity. It begins with the individual and the personal qualities that need to be developed. The three qualities are the Consciousness of Self, Congruence, and Commitment. Under each quality there are the "seven C's" which are outlined below.

The first focus area, Consciousness of Self, refers to "the beliefs, values, attitudes, and emotions that motivate one to take action" (Higher Education Research Institute, 1996, p. 31). Consciousness of Self is knowing oneself and being self-aware (i.e., knowing your personality, talents, interests, aspirations, etc.). The Higher Education Research Institute contends that leaders need to be self-aware before they can lead others.

Congruence refers to thinking, feeling, and behaving with consistency, genuineness, authenticity, and honesty toward others (Higher Education Research Institute, 1996, p. 36). People who are congruent are those whose actions are consistent with their beliefs and intentions. This quality clearly depends upon an established consciousness of self.

Commitment refers to "the psychic energy that motivates the individual to serve and that drives the collective effort. Commitment implies passion, intensity, and duration" (Higher Education Research Institute, 1996, p. 40). It helps the group find a common purpose and formulate effective strategies within that purpose as well as sustain the group during times of controversy. Here, one's consciousness of self and desire to live congruently lead to one's commitment to serve with and for others.

The second focus area of the Social Change Model is the group. How can the collaborative leadership development process be designed to facilitate development in this area? This includes Collaboration, Common Purpose, and Controversy with Civility.

Collaboration involves the ability "to work with others in a common effort. It constitutes the cornerstone value of the group leadership effort because it empowers self and others through trust" (Higher Education Research Institute, 1996 p. 48). Mattessich and Monsey (as quoted in Higher Education Research Institute) define collaboration as "a mutually beneficial and well-defined relationship that includes a commitment to a definition of goals; a jointly developed structure and shared responsibility; mutual authority and accountability for success; and sharing not only of responsibilities but also of the rewards" (p. 48). By having consciousness of self, congruency, and commitment, a person is in a position to seek collaboration with a group.

Common Purpose refers to "work with shared aims and values. It facilitates the group's ability to engage in collective analysis of the issues at hand and the task to be undertaken" (Higher Education Research Institute, 1996, p.55). Common purpose is best achieved when all members in the group share in the same vision, purpose, and goals that the group is working toward. To reach common purpose, the individual has to be self-aware, congruent in his or her decisions, committed to the task at hand, and be willing to work collaboratively with others.

Controversy with Civility "recognizes two fundamental realities of any creative group effort: that differences in viewpoint are inevitable, and that such difference must be aired openly but with civility" (Higher Education Research Institute, 1996, p. 59). Resolving these differences with civility makes it easier for all group members to work together more effectively. The Higher Education Research Institute stated, "Controversy, in short, is viewed as an inevitable part of group interaction which can reinforce the other values in the model if it occurs in an atmosphere of civility" (p. 60).

The third and final focus area is the community and society. To what social ends is the leadership development activity directed? The focus here is Citizenship.

Citizenship is "the process whereby the individual and the collaborative group become responsibly connected to the community and the society through the leadership development activity" (Higher Education Research Institute, 1996, p. 65). Citizenship is the final goal of this leadership development model. According to the Higher Education Research Institute, "It serves to underscore the fact that the social change toward which any leadership activity is directed is ultimately intended for the betterment of others and the larger community/society" (p. 65). Citizenship leads to change, which is the purpose of this model and all leadership development models. According to the Higher Education Research Institute, change is the hub that gives meaning and purpose to the seven Cs. The ultimate goal of the creative process of leadership is to bring about the change that will make a better world and society for self as well as others.

Emotionally Intelligent Leadership
Copyright © 2008
Marcy Levy Shankman and Scott J. Allen

Consider exploring *Emotionally Intelligent Leadership* (EIL) for your leadership development program. EIL was developed by Dr. Marcy Shankman and Dr. Scott Allen in 2008. This model is a great foundation for your leadership development efforts because it provides a simple, educational approach to leadership.

The premise of Emotional Intelligent Leadership is looking at leadership through three different lenses. The first is Consciousness of Self, which refers to being "self-aware." As identified in this book, leadership starts with yourself. If you don't know your own strengths and weaknesses and if you don't understand your own personality and leadership styles, how can you expect to understand and lead others?

The second component is Context, the environment around you. This is referred to as "getting on the balcony." We must teach leaders to be aware of the people they are leading and where they are leading them to. Leaders must be trained to step back and observe how people are acting in a given situation. This is an important concept which is often not put into practice.

Finally, Allen & Shankman outline Consciousness of Others: being aware of your relationships and the specific talents and abilities that each team member can contribute. Are students able to meet their team half way? A leader has to understand that everyone brings different perspectives to the table. This is why leadership is so complex, but also exciting. A leader must learn how to work with everyone on their team while keeping the end goal in mind.

The Leadership Challenge
Copyright © 2012
James M. Kouzes and Barry Z. Posner

The Leadership Challenge "is about how leaders mobilize others to want to make extraordinary things happen in organizations" (p. 2). Kouzes and Posner (2012) challenge us to put values into actions, visions into realities, obstacles into innovations, separateness into solidarity, and risks into rewards.

Kouzes and Posner (2012) break the Leadership Challenge into five practices. 1) Model the Way, 2) Inspire a Shared Vision, 3) Challenge the Process, 4) Enable Others to Act, and 5) Encourage the Heart.

Model the Way: "The first step a leader must take along the path to becoming an exemplary leader is inward. It's a step toward discovering personal values and beliefs. Leaders must find their voice. They must find the principles that guide decisions and actions" (Kouzes and Posner, p. 42).

Inspire a Shared Vision: "Leaders must envision the future by imagining exciting and ennobling possibilities. They should enlist others by appealing to shared aspirations" (Kouzes and Posner, p. 100).

Challenge the Process: "Leaders must search for opportunities by seizing the initiative and looking outward for innovative ways to improve. They should experiment and take risks by constantly generating small wins and learning from experiences" (Kouzes and Posner, p. 156).

Enable Others to Act: "Leaders must foster collaboration by building trust and facilitating relationships. They should be able to strengthen others by increasing self-determination and developing competence" (Kouzes and Posner, p. 214).

Encourage the Heart: "Leaders must recognize contributions by showing appreciation for individual excellence. They should celebrate the values and victories by creating a spirit of community" (Kouzes and Posner, p. 272).

Frameworks

Frameworks give structure by providing an outline or format that can guide your leadership programming. Below are several frameworks to consider.

Zing!
Copyright © 2004
Nancy Hunter Denney

Nancy Hunter Denney brings us *Zing!* in *How to Zing! Your Life & Leadership*, 2004. A single word speaks volumes in the *Zing!* approach to life and leadership. Created and trademarked by Nancy Hunter Denney in *Zing! Insights on Maximizing Your Influence*, the word *Zing!* (exclamation point required) represents the "ability to overcome competing forces to positively influence others towards a greater social good." Leaders are empowered to focus on being present, fully aware, and engaged in their surroundings so they can positively influence others by making them feel worthy in their presence. Three things are needed to be a leader with *Zing!*: a willingness to act, the ability to work in collaboration with others, and a growing personal magnetism.

Zing! encourages the leader to ask "how" not "if," and to be willing to take risks. The ability to inspire, direct, and work with others is an essential condition of leadership. *Zing!* leaders ask, "How can I help?" and look for ways to contribute to their immediate surroundings on a daily basis. Serving others without the need for recognition demonstrates the giving spirit of a leader with *Zing!*. Seeing others clearly, listening intently, and being fully present allows the leader to build trust, demonstrate commitment, and be a source of hope and optimism.

This framework encourages leaders to recognize that influence does not happen in a vacuum. Using the *Zing!* Impact Equation, Denney notes the obstacles associated with forwarding a mission or serving the greater social good. The equation states that one's potential to influence is a function of "the person" plus their "environment of opportunity" plus the use of 21 specific skills called "insights" minus "individual detractors." Individual detractors are behaviors like speaking negatively of others, arriving late or being the first to leave a meeting, bringing hidden agendas into one's role, using discriminatory language, finishing other's sentences, and other behaviors that counter the skills and attitudes necessary to be a great leader.

The use of 21 Insights, on the other hand, enhances the potential influence of a leader because they are learn-able skills like adaptability, interpersonal communication, self-exploration, and adventurousness. These Insights are listed below and on the following page:

The Opportunity of Self-Inspection – Insight One

The Content of Character – Insight Two

The Power of Purpose – Insight Three

The Inspiration of Vision – Insight Four

The Transcending of Adversity – Insight Five

The Face of Courage – Insight Six

The Plus of Adaptability – Insight Seven

The Positives of Attitude – Insight Eight

The Magnetism of Praise – Insight Nine

The Rules of Respect – Insight Ten

The Necessity of Nourishment – Insight Eleven

The Draw of Intelligence – Insight Twelve

The Example Setting of Determination – Insight Thirteen

The Art of Interpersonal Communication – Insight Fourteen

The Attraction of Listening – Insight Fifteen

The Pull of the Podium – Insight Sixteen

The Building of Relationships – Insight Seventeen

The Punch of Humor – Insight Eighteen

The Appeal of Playfulness – Insight Nineteen

The Gift of Self-Discipline – Insight Twenty

The Hand of Humility – Insight Twenty-One

To summarize, *Zing!* can be described as being colorful, never beige. Zing! is the "it" you wish you had when you needed it most in group settings. When leaders know it's always "Zing! time," they finally understand the potential power in being fully present.

Greater Than Yourself
Copyright © 2009
Extreme Leadership with Steve Farber

"Greater Than Yourself" (GTY) was created by Steven Farber, 2009. The concept is simple: "pay it forward." Leaders must help their followers become better leaders than themselves.

Leadership is about creating change, and GTY is a change process. Farber promotes challenging students to take on a GTY project. This is a great opportunity to immerse your students in their community while putting their skills to practice. Through community service, students come to a deeper understanding of leadership and learn to be effective communicators. At some point in your leadership program you could consider providing the opportunity for students to put their skills to practice by having them take on a GTY project.

Theories

The Handbook for Student Leadership Development states that "theory provides the overarching sense-making frame for experience. Without a theoretical framework to connect and integrate experiences there is no sense-making, and thus there can be no learning" (Komives, Dugan, Owen, Slack, and Wagner, 2011, p. 35).

Below is sampling of theories to consider. If you find something that intrigues you and would fit into your leadership program, spend time reviewing the literature on that particular theory.

Meyers-Briggs Type Indicator
www.myersbriggs.org

Myers and Myers (1980) developed the Myers-Briggs personality assessment based on Carl Jung's theory of personality type. According to Evans, Forney, and Guido-DiBrito (1998), the "personality type theory focuses on how people use perception and judgment" (p. 245).

The result of the Myers-Briggs Type Indicator is to identify four preferences: (a) extroversion or introversion, (b) sensing or intuition, (c) thinking or feeling, and (d) judgment or perception. Once people know more about their own personalities, they can start to identify how they prefer to operate, and better learn how to interact with people with different personalities. It is important to recognize that no one type is better than another. People should rec-

The Eight Preferences

Where you prefer to focus your attention

E **Extraversion**
People who prefer Extraversion tend to focus their attention on the outer world of people and things.

Introversion **I**
People who prefer Introversion tend to focus their attention on the inner world of ideas and expression.

The way your prefer to take in infomation

S **Sensing**
People who prefer Sensing tend to take in information through the five senses and focus on the here and now.

Intuition **N**
People who prefer Intuition tend to take in information from patterns and the big picture and focus on future possibilities.

The way your prefer to make decisions

T **Thinking**
People who prefer Thinking tend to make decisions based primarily on logic and on objective analysis of cause and effect.

Feeling **F**
People who prefer Feeling tend to make decisions based primarily on values and on subjective evaluation person-centered concerns.

How your prefer to deal with the outer world

J **Judging**
People who prefer Judging tend to like a planned and organized approach to life and prefer to have things settled.

Perceiving **P**
People who prefer Perceiving tend to like a flexible and spontaneous approach to life and prefer to keep their options open.

ognize the different personalities and learn how to balance them out when working together.

This self-assessment tool identifies dominant personality traits. When developing leaders, it is our job to help them understand what they need to develop weaker traits that will help them become well-rounded leaders. Before you use this tool in your leadership program, it is recommended that you seek training on how to facilitate a workshop of this nature.

Myers-Briggs Type Indicator® and MBTI®

Authentic Leadership
Copyright © 2003
William George

Authentic Leadership is defined as "a process that draws from both positive psychological capacities and a highly developed organizational context, which results in both greater self-awareness and self-regulated positive behaviors on the part of leaders and associates, fostering positive self-development (Avolio, Walumbwa, and Weber, 2009, p. 423).

In the book *Authentic Leadership: Rediscovering the Secrets to Creating a Lasting Value*, Bill George (2003) outlines that authentic leaders:

- Understand their purpose

- Practice solid values

- Lead with heart

- Establish connected relationships

- Demonstrate self-discipline (p. 18)

According to George (2003), "Authentic leaders genuinely desire to serve others through their leadership. They are more interested in empowering the people they lead to make a difference than they are in power, money, or prestige for themselves" (p. 12).

Tuckman's Group Development

In 1965, Bruce Tuckman developed a theory which looked at stages of group development.

According to Komives, Lucas, and McMahon (1998), Tuckman initially developed a four-stage model of group development and, after further research, added a fifth stage.

1. **Forming**: The first stage refers to the initial coming together of the group and involves such tasks as member recruitment and affiliation (Komives, Lucas, McMahon, 1998). In this stage, team members get to know one another, begin to take on different roles, and begin to develop some initial goals.

2. **Storming**: In order to move forward as a group, the members must be willing to address genuine conflicts and disagreements within the team. It is important at this stage to get any differences that may exist on the table and work them out before moving forward. According to Komives et al. (1998), "If the group is not clear about its purposes and goals, or if the group cannot agree on shared goals, then it might collapse" (p. 168).

3. **Norming**: At this time, according to Komives et

al. (1998), "the group sets up formal and informal procedures for which things come to the whole group, which reports are needed, who is involved in what, and how people interact" (p. 169). The members start to work together in a more consistent and effective manner.

4. Performing: "Built on the strong foundation of the previous stages, the group now cycles into a mature stage of equilibrium—getting its work done" (Komives et al., 1998, p. 170).

5. Adjourning: The final stage involves bringing the group or task to a close. This is when the group ends a task and leaves relationships that were formed.

Additional Theories to Explore:

Complexity Leadership

Leadership: Current Theories, Research, and Future Directions (Avoli, Walumbwa, and Weber, 2009), states that "leadership is viewed as an interactive system of dynamic, unpredictable agents that interact with each other in complex feedback networks, which can then produce adaptive outcomes such as knowledge dissemination, learning, innovation, and further adaptation to change" (p. 430).

Leader-Member Exchange (LMX)

Leadership: Current Theories, Research, and Future Directions (Avoli, Walumbwa, and Weber, 2009). LMX focuses on the relationship between the leader and the follower. The central principle of LMX theory is that "leaders develop different exchange relationships with their followers, whereby the quality of the relationship alters the impact on important leader and member outcomes. Thus, leadership occurs when leaders and followers are able to develop effective relationships that result in mutual and incremental influence" (p. 433).

Servant Leadership

Servant Leadership was coined by Robert K. Greenleaf in *The Servant as Leader* (1970). "The servant-leader is servant first. It begins with the natural feeling that one wants to serve, to serve first. Then conscious choice brings one to aspire to lead. That person is sharply different from one who is leader first, perhaps because of the need to assuage an unusual power drive or to acquire material possessions" (Greenleaf, p. 14).

A servant leader's primary focus is on a person's growth and well-being. A servant leader shares the power and puts the needs of others first.

Transformational Leadership

James MacGregor Burns first brought the concept of *"Transformational Leadership"* to prominence in his book *Leadership*. Transformational leadership is "a process where leaders and followers raise one another to higher levels of morality and motivation" (Komives, Lucas, McMahan 1998).

Situational Leadership II

Check out Dr. Ken Blanchard's book, *Leadership and the One Minute Manager: Increasing Effectiveness through Situational Leadership II*, 2013.

Seven Habits of Highly Effective People

Another great resource is Stephen R. Covey's book *The 7 Habits of Highly Effective People: Powerful Lessons in Personal Change*, 1989.

Conclusion

Determining the most valuable leadership theories, models, and frameworks to apply to your programs can be extremely overwhelming, especially if you have limited familiarity with the literature on leadership theory. This chapter includes a sampling of what's out there. Practitioners should further explore these and other theories, models, and frameworks to determine which ones will best fit your campus programs. The objective of this book is to provide a foundation and get you started on exploring different theories that may be applicable to your leadership programs.

CHAPTER 6

A Sampling of Leadership Programs and Models

There are hundreds of leadership programs across the country. Some have structured programs, while others offer a variety of unconnected opportunities for their students. It is up to you as a practitioner to decide whether you want to create a structured, formal leadership program. "Formal leadership programs are intentionally designed learning opportunities aimed at expanding college student's knowledge, skills, and values" (Dugan, Bohle, Gebhardt, Hofert, Wilk, and Cooney, 2011, p. 66). A formal program offers students a related set of experiences that moves from basic to advanced leadership skills.

According to Dugan et al. "experiences such as internships, interactions across and about difference, mentoring relationships, group and team engagement, and community service have all demonstrated measurable influence on leadership development" (p. 75).

In *The Handbook for Student Leadership Development*, (Komives, Dugan, Owen, Slack, Wagner, 2011) suggest three types of student leadership programs to consider.

- *"Formal leadership program:* An intentional collection of leadership experiences that are integrated into an overall experience designed with the purpose of developing or enhancing leadership skills, knowledge, and capacity.

- *Individual leadership experience:* An element of a leadership program intentionally designed to develop leadership capacity. This experience, such as a course or retreat, when combined with other experiences comprise the various dimensions of a formal leadership program, but may also serve as stand-alone experiences unattached to a greater whole.

- *Leadership activity:* A specific event or activity that exists within the context of the individual leadership experience. The activity such as leadership inventory, assignment, or discussion, is intentionally aligned with the leadership goals of the individual leadership experience and larger formal leadership program" (p. 232).

The remainder of this chapter will highlight seven leadership programs from across the country. Remember, this is just a sampling.

Canisius College
www.canisius.edu/campus-life/cpld/leadership-development

The Leadership Development Program at Canisius College provides opportunities for students to expand their leadership skills and sense of civic responsibility. Their programs, like the LEAD Team, enhance the Canisius experience by preparing students for lifelong leadership roles.

Objectives

- Place the Jesuit principles of Canisius College into the context of lifelong leadership.

- Offer a variety of training programs that enhance leadership skills.

- Provide a varied program that responds to the diverse needs of all participants.

- Assist students in developing their own personal leadership style.

- Engage students in reflective discussion/exercises about their own leadership experiences in regards to their values, morals, ethics, and beliefs.

- Train students to facilitate leadership development programs for their peers.

- Facilitate interaction between student leaders and community members to foster the concept of leadership as service beyond self.

- Explore the Social Change model as a foundation of leadership development.

- Empower students to become advocates for and agents of change.

Programs and Retreats

Canisius Leadership Institute

The Canisius Leadership Institute (CLI) is a comprehensive leadership development program based on the Social Change Model of leadership development. Through a multifaceted approach to learning leadership, students within the institute will hone and perfect various leadership skills and attributes.

The CLI is comprised of four certification levels:

- Emerging Leaders - these are students who are just beginning their leadership experience. These leaders are new to the role of leadership, and are prone to make the most mistakes. Some good skills for this level would be time management, organization, etc.

- Established Leaders - these students have gone through one or two leadership roles. They have made their initial mistakes, and hopefully learned from them. They are now beginning to think globally about their leadership positions, focusing on not only their organization but the campus community as well.

- Experienced Leaders - these are students who are veteran leaders, and are beginning to think about sharing their experiences with potential leaders. These students begin to reflect on their leadership experiences, and evaluate themselves as effective leaders.

- Capstone Leaders - This is the highest level of leadership. These leaders have truly evaluated who they are as leaders, and have grown into effective role models for up and coming leaders. They think globally about not only the campus community, but the surrounding community as well. These leaders begin to evaluate how they will fit in the world, and start to create their visions of change.

Empire Creativity Competition

The Empire Creativity Competition presents teams of students with an opportunity to pitch their business idea to a panel of judges and a chance to win cash prizes. Ideas may be at any stage of development from creation of concepts or ideas to an established business.

Leadership Retreat

Students learn to lead and inspire others at the Student Leadership Retreat. Topics explored include ethics, beliefs and values, personal leadership philosophies, and spirituality. All Canisius College undergraduate students are encouraged to participate in this enlightening retreat experience.

Leadership Series

The Leadership Series offers student leaders and the Canisius community a unique opportunity to learn leadership lessons and gain inspiration through proven leaders in society as well as those with an important message.

Student Leadership Conference

This annual student leadership conference is designed to introduce Canisius students to the different aspects of leadership while allowing current student leaders the chance to hone their leadership skills.

LEAD Team

LEAD Team (Leaders Educating and Developing) facilitators work closely with Campus Programming & Leadership Development (CPLD) to assist in the development, coordination, promotion, and implementation of workshops designed to promote leadership skills and ideals. LEAD Team members are trained to serve as facilitators of team-building exercises and leadership development workshops. All members plan, present, and evaluate leadership workshops for their peers.

High School Leadership Workshop

The High School Leadership Workshop takes place annually during the summer months. Workshop sessions enlist student's active participation rather than lecturing or one-sided presentations. The agenda for the day includes individual and group exercises that focus on the skills necessary for problem solving, communication skill building, strategies of motivation, and goal setting techniques. This program is open to high school students from Western New York who are nominated to attend by their Guidance Counselor.

Bowling Green State University
www2.bgsu.edu/offices/sa/leadership/

The BGSU Leadership Certificate Program is a self-paced and comprehensive leadership development program designed to encourage and recognize student leadership education and experiences at Bowling Green State University.

The program is adaptable so all students can work toward achieving this distinguished recognition. To participate, students must answer yes to the following questions:

- Are you interested in improving your leadership skills and abilities?

- Are you or will you be an active student leader at BGSU?

- Do you have a cumulative GPA of 2.5 or higher?

- Are you committed to giving back through community service?

The BGSU Leadership Certificate Program Advantage

- Demonstrates student's leadership and team development skills

- Highlights developmental outcomes of each leadership experience

- Assists students as they transition to leadership and team roles within a work environment

The BGSU Leadership Certificate Program Requirements

- Leadership Education Experiences

  - Leadership and program workshops

  - Academic course work

  - Leadership conferences or seminars

- Leadership Mentoring

  - Provided by BGSU faculty and staff

- Community Service Experience

  - Volunteering for service hours

  - Assist with planning and coordinating service projects

- Practical Leadership Experiences

  - BGSU student organization projects and events

  - BGSU student employment projects and events

  - Co-ops, internships and practicum projects and events

  - Leadership projects

Fall Semester

Student Leader Retreat: The Student Leader Retreat (SLR) has a strong tradition of bringing prominent BGSU student groups together to highlight the importance of their roles on campus. This 2 1/2-day experience is designed to build a foundation for a year of successful collaboration around student events, programs and projects.

Leadership Academy: Leadership Academy is the premier, annual leadership conference at Bowling Green State University. This one-day event takes place in November and engages students in educational sessions targeted toward their leadership development. Participants have the opportunity to explore personal and leadership values, network with other campus leaders, and develop the skills necessary for success.

Falcon Leadership Institute: The Center for Leadership's Falcon Leadership Institute develops self-aware leaders who have the skills to build professional networks and create personal connections within their cohort and throughout campus. Guided by the ideals of servant leadership, students participate in service-learning and leadership projects that enhance the community. Participants begin earning the BGSU Leadership Certificate by learning the skills and competencies necessary for a successful life and career.

Spring Semester

Leadership Week: The Annual Leadership Week will celebrate and promote leadership across BGSU's campus through discussions, presentations, and information sessions. This week-long initiative will feature programs to get students involved and learning more about leadership opportunities and what being a leader at BGSU is all about.

Leadership Legacy Series: The Center for Leadership presents the annual Student Leadership Legacy Series. This series will be comprised of six different sessions throughout April presented by graduating BGSU student leaders. These students will select topics centered on areas that have been most helpful to them during their leadership journey.

The LeaderShape Institute: The LeaderShape® Institute is an intensive and energizing six-day program designed to encourage participants to become leaders with integrity. The curriculum is used on college campuses nationwide and participants become alumni of this prestigious program.

Geneseo
gold.geneseo.edu

Also check out Tom Matthews, *Building Leaders One Hour at a Time: Guidebook for Leadership Development*, 2013.

The Geneseo Opportunities for Leadership Development program seeks to prepare students for leadership roles and responsibilities in service to college and the global community. Their mission is accomplished through education, development, and training of students in an extensive series of personal development programs, institutes, leadership certificates, service learning, volunteer work, and active engagement in college and community life.

Bronze Life Skills Certificate: The Bronze Certificate provides an introduction to new perspectives on leaders and leadership, suggests pathways for personal growth and development, and offers a range of individual and group leadership and life skills. The Bronze Certificate will be awarded upon completion of eight workshops, including the four required workshops (Leadership Concepts, Personal Development Session, Listening Skills & Presentation Skills), and submission of journal reflections for each workshop.

Silver Practicing Leadership Certificate: The Silver Certificate offers additional skill development, assists students in higher level group development, explores the range of personal learning and leadership styles, and helps students discover their strengths and effective leadership practices. The Silver Certificate will be awarded upon completion of the Bronze Certificate and eight of workshops, including the four required workshops (Team-building, Running Effective Meetings, Leadership Styles & Leadership Practices Inventory), and submission of journal reflections for each workshop.

Gold Personal Leadership Model Certificate: The Gold Certificate provides opportunities to explore a wide variety of leadership theories and models in the context of the historical development of leadership as an emerging field of study, examines individual leadership theories, assists students in developing a personal leadership model, and requires students to demonstrate an understanding of a minimum of eight of the major leadership theories. The Gold designated theory workshops may not be offered every semester.

Sapphire Volunteerism and Service Leadership Certificate: The Sapphire Certificate is designed to help students involved in volunteering recognize and understand the opportunities, responsibilities, service, and leadership performed by volunteers for the greater good of society. The Sapphire Certificate program provides a conceptual framework for volunteerism, offers basic information on the do's and don'ts of volunteering, offers skill-building training, encourages reflection on the experiences, and introduces a range of theoretical models of volunteerism and leadership.

The Sapphire Certificate will be awarded upon completion of eight workshops, including the four required workshops (Volunteerism, Engagement & Service, Rights and Responsibilities of Volunteers, Volunteer Fair Participation & Volunteer Involvement Reflections) and submission of journal reflections for each workshop, and evidence of twenty hours of volunteer work or participation in service learning projects.

Opal Diversity and Cultural Competency Certificate: The Opal Certificate is designed to help students recognize and understand that all environments are diverse and that diverse environments are complex and challenging, present a wealth of opportunity, and are constantly changing. Students will be introduced to the skill sets needed to be better able to address the challenges, as well as recognize and mine the opportunities that diversity presents. Upon completion of the program, the student will be: more comfortable working as a member of a diverse team; better able to recognize cross-cultural barriers that can hinder communication; and less likely to make assumptions about others based on superficial traits and characteristics.

The Opal Certificate will be awarded upon completion of eight workshops, including the four required workshops (Making the Case for Cultural Competency, Identity Expression, Cross-Cultural Problem Solving & Taking the Next Steps) and submission of journal reflections for each workshop.

Emerald Career and Professional Development Certificate: The Emerald Certificate has been designed to help students develop and apply lifelong career development skills to the world of work as a student employee or a full time career professional, or both. Students will learn strategies to navigate workplace issues, develop an awareness of appropriate behavior in professional settings, and prepare for the transition to a career after college. Workshops will provide opportunities to enhance personal and professional skills that are workplace expectations and help prepare students for promotions and higher level supervisory positions.

The Emerald Certificate will be awarded upon completion of eight workshops, including the four required workshops (Exploring Your Future Through the Strong Interest Inventory, Interviewing Skills, Finding an Internship, and Preparing Your Resume) and submission of journal reflections for each workshop.

Ruby Certificate for Information Management and Digital Age Leadership: The Ruby Certificate program is designed to help students become discerning members of the information society, able to find and evaluate information quickly and with confidence. Upon completion of the program students will be: able to sift through the massive amounts of information thrown at us in this society; capable of evaluating sources of information for accuracy and relevancy; confident in their ability to do solid research crucial to the decision making process; and aware of the ethical issues involving the use of information. Though particularly useful for students in their first and second years of college, these skills will help anyone save precious time by increasing efficiency in their personal and professional lives.

Diamond Civic Engagement Certificate: The Diamond Civic Engagement Leadership Certificate is designed to prepare students for lifelong engagement and involvement in community life through individual and collective actions designed to identify and address issues of public concern. Students will need to utilize many of the leadership skills offered in the Bronze, Silver, Emerald and Sapphire certificates to successfully complete this certificate. Civic engagement begins with volunteering and service and requires a higher level of commitment that involves working with others in a campus or community-based project or social justice issue. Engagement includes joining neighborhood organizations; participating in local school and community organizations; joining political parties and running for office; active involvement in local, state, national and global organizations and issues; and serving others to make a positive difference in the local, regional, national and global community.

Jade Leadership in Sustainability Certificate: The Jade Certificate is designed to help students recognize the importance of sustainability issues in their personal and professional lives and to understand their responsibilities as individuals and community members to promote and encourage sustainable practices. The Jade certificate provides both a theoretical and practical foundation for students looking to take on leadership roles in the movement to build a more sustainable society.

Platinum Certificate: Students who earn all nine (9) certificates will also be awarded a Platinum Certificate in recognition of their commitment and involvement in leadership development through the GOLD Program.

Marquette University
www.marquette.edu/osd/leadership

Marquette University strives to develop men and women with a capacity for leadership expressed in service to others.

The process of leadership is practiced and learned through a number of experiential activities and roles: employment, community service, student organizations, and coursework all contribute to knowledge and understanding of leadership. Recently, the Division of Student Affairs unveiled a new model of student leadership development that puts leadership in a context unique to Marquette's mission. This model forms the basis for student leadership training experiences across the Division.

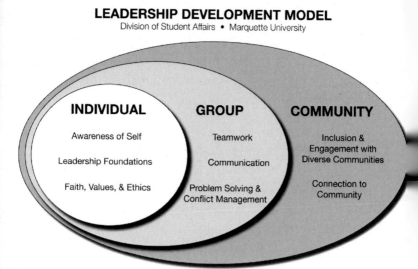

LEADERSHIP DEVELOPMENT MODEL
Division of Student Affairs • Marquette University

INDIVIDUAL
Awareness of Self
Leadership Foundations
Faith, Values, & Ethics

GROUP
Teamwork
Communication
Problem Solving & Conflict Management

COMMUNITY
Inclusion & Engagement with Diverse Communities
Connection to Community

Leadership Experiences

One-Time Leadership Development Experiences

- Student Organization Leader Institute

Ongoing Leadership Development Experiences

- Ignatian Leadership Retreat

- Students Taking Active Roles - STAR (first-semester freshman)

- Companions in Leadership

Other Leadership Links

- Team-building Facilitators

- Division of Student Affairs Leadership Awards

The College at Brockport State University of New York
www.brockport.edu/leadership

At the College at Brockport, formal opportunities for leadership development are provided through a developmentally sequenced, co-curricular certificate program based primarily on the Social Change Model of Leadership. The Leadership Development Program offers students the opportunity to engage in a variety of experiences that have been shown to have a significant impact on students' leadership capacity and self-efficacy. The program utilizes the following methods to encourage leadership development in a diverse world:

- Engaging workshops and seminars

- Mentoring relationships with faculty, staff and students

- Ongoing opportunities for community service

- Discussions with peers about issues of diversity, privilege and social justice

- Social action projects within the community

- Annual leadership conference, planned by Capstone Certificate participants that allows students to develop relationships with Brockport alumni who serve as session presenters

University of Rhode Island
web.uri.edu/leadership/lcp

The Leadership Certificate Program is a competency based 3-tier co-curricular leadership program grounded in experiential learning and leadership theory. Members of the LCP cohorts participate in programs to help sharpen natural strengths and develop essential leadership skills. Members are able to structure the program around their individual schedules and interests to enhance their URI experience. Each competency has similar requirements to obtain a certificate in that specific skill area. Once members have completed certificates in at least 3 individual competencies, they are eligible to complete the requirements to become a Leadership Coach. Competencies include: *Experiential & Adventure-Based Education, Cultural Competence,* and *Mentoring & Coaching.*

Each competency starts with an opening retreat at the beginning of each semester, designed to provide an introduction to the competency, build community among cohort members, and develop learning plans with coaches in order to create a memorable and marketable series of experiences. Once cohort members have completed their skill building experiences, they must participate in an approved facilitation skills training and accompanying program facilitation within their given competency. This allows for cohort members to apply learned skills. Cohort members are also required to attend the CSLD's Professional Development event held once a year, as well as the closing LCP celebration.

Experiential and Adventure-Based Education

As a result of successfully completing the experiential and adventure based education competency, it is expected that you will be able to:

- Co-create programming around personal and group responsibility, problem solving, self-discovery, and team building

- Effectively analyze group development process and dynamics to create positive change within group performance

- Think critically in order to solve complex problems

- Understand the interrelationships and interconnections within groups and organizations

- Perform processing/debriefing discussions at the close of activities using a variety of different techniques

- Utilize social skills necessary for effective communication, teamwork and leadership

- Speak and present effectively in front of small and large audiences

University of Virginia

www.virginia.edu/deanofstudents/programsandservices/leadership.html

The University of Virginia targets its programs to students at three developmental levels: *Aspiring/Emerging, Engaging*, and *Excelling/Mentoring.*

Aspiring/Emerging

Focuses on program components that build or reinforce foundational knowledge, analytical skills, and problem solving competencies, assuming that the participants have not had considerable prior experience in these areas.

Programs include:

The Blueprint Emerging Leaders Program: Blueprint is a program designed for First and Second Year students and transfer students who demonstrate leadership potential and aspire to develop their personal and organizational leadership skills. The program is designed to provide students with a strong leadership knowledge base and focuses on five core components:

- Discovering Individual Strengths

- Communication & Conflict Management

- Leadership & Follower-ship

- Student Self-Governance

- Citizen Leadership & Global Stewardship

Women's Leadership Development Program: The Women's Leadership Development Program provides undergraduate women with leadership skills through a series of workshops and speakers. Students who exhibit leadership potential are nominated for the program by fellow students, faculty, and/or staff.

APALTI: The Asian Pacific American Training Institute (APALTI) is a student-facilitated, culturally aware leadership development program designed to build confidence, enhance competence, and strengthen connectedness among a selected group of first and second-year Asian and Asian Pacific American students at UVA. By helping these students discover their personal leadership style, the program aims to increase participation of A/APAs in community wide leadership roles.

Engaging

Focuses on those students who have plugged into a student organization and are looking to learn contextualized content that can apply to their particular involvement.

Programs include:

Student Leadership Network: A virtual network housed on the UVA site open to any student currently involved in leadership activities around the Grounds. The site provides resources and information as well as opportunities for virtual networking, discussion boards, and information about events, speakers and other activities of interest to student leaders.

DiAPAson Leadership Retreat: DiAPAson serves as a half-day retreat for executive board members of organizations, highlighting all the resources UVA has to offer student leaders. This event also provides team building activities in order to create and nurture relationships among student leaders to facilitate collaboration in the future.

WAALI: Through structured weekly conversation over the course of the fall semester, the Women's Asian American Leadership Initiative provides a small group of 2nd and 3rd year women the chance to share and learn strategies for personal and professional success as Asian Pacific American women at UVA and beyond.

The Leadership & Organizational Development Conference for Multicultural Students: The purpose of the LODC is to provide student leaders with the necessary skills and tools to lead their organizations effectively. Come build your leadership portfolio! We accomplish this purpose through a networking session, guest speaker, student-leader panel, and a series of workshop offerings.

Excelling/Mentoring

Focuses on those students who are continuing to build upon their leadership knowledge while empowering and working to develop the future leaders of their organizations. In addition, these students are beginning to think about their leadership experiences and how they may help to enhance and even define their future career aspirations.

Programs include:

Leadership 2K (L2K): Leadership 2000 is an intensive one-week summer program for the leaders of major, University-wide organizations designed to enhance their skills, increase their knowledge of the University, extend their network of University contacts, and contribute to a sense of community among student leaders. Sponsored by the Offices of the Vice President and Chief Student Affairs Officer and the Dean of Students, its purpose is to support student leaders and their organizations as they assume the major responsibilities associated with self-governance. The program topics and activities vary by year, but have in the past included: case studies in leadership, effective and ethical decision-making, diversity, exemplary leadership, delegation, motivation and empowerment, facilitation, and setting priorities. Students are also introduced to key University representatives and participate in discussions about the University's goals, plans, and challenges. Participation is by invitation.

Atlantic Coast Athletic Conference International al Academic Collaborative (ACCIAC) Leadership Conference: Student leaders from the 12 ACC Colleges and Universities have the opportunity to learn through intensive engagement in educational sessions, keynote addresses, topical content exploration, simulations, and experiential application. Five-to-seven student leaders are selected from UVA each year to participate and meet leaders from the other ACC schools while building upon their leadership skills and learning to collaborate across institutions.

A/APA President's Planning Retreat: The A/APA President's Planning Retreat is a half-day retreat for presidents of the A/APA organizations. This event provides presidents the opportunity to interact with other leaders and share challenges as well as successes. Team-building and training workshops are determined based on participant interest and need.

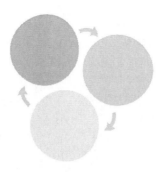

CHAPTER 7

Parkinson's Leadership Development Program

Do you ever wonder why people are mesmerized by some works of art, but not interested in others? You seem to get the point. You seem to understand what the artist is trying to communicate and take the time to consider what, if anything, the artist is trying to draw out of you, the observer. Your ability to see what others might not see exists because you view life through the lens of an educator. You are in a position to help students identify who they are and what they can be. You put the pieces in place and encourage, support, challenge, and teach.

Up to this point, this book has identified and discussed the tools needed to create a comprehensive leadership development program. While the importance of bringing yourself through the process is extremely central to philosophy, you don't always have to re-invent the wheel. Spend your time and energy plugging your ideas into a framework or model that works, instead of spending hours staring at a blank "canvas" or more realistically, a very still computer screen!

Leadership development quickly became a passion of mine as a student affairs professional in 1999. I began as the Coordinator of Programs and Resident Director at a small private business university in New England. Three years later, I became the Assistant Director of Student Activities, responsible for the student programming board, leadership development, and new student orientation. Given my growing interest in leadership and my experience in student programming, I pursued a doctoral degree in higher education and leadership. My research focused on investigating comprehensive models for leadership development programming. Seeking to synthesize the best of my research and my personal experience, I developed the Parkinson's Leadership Development Program (PLDP).

The PLDP is one way in which you can plan, organize and implement a comprehensive leadership development program for college students. College practitioners can utilize components of this program that fit the mission of their leadership program and institution.

Overview of the PLDP

The PLDP leads students through a three-stage process:

Emerge, Develop, and Advance. Each stage develops a specific set of skills that are essential to being a successful leader. The effectiveness of the PLDP is rooted in the diversity of delivery methods used. The methods include retreats, institutes, conferences, workshops, speakers, traveling workshops, and service learning opportunities. All programs incorporate experiential learning techniques which are grounded in leadership theory. The various methods correspond to the many learning styles and needs of your students.

Chapters 8-10 offer a detailed look at each stage of the PLDP, but before exploring each stage, it is important to define the different delivery methods that are used throughout:

Retreat. A retreat is an opportunity to train for a weekend to promote learning and enhance specific skills.

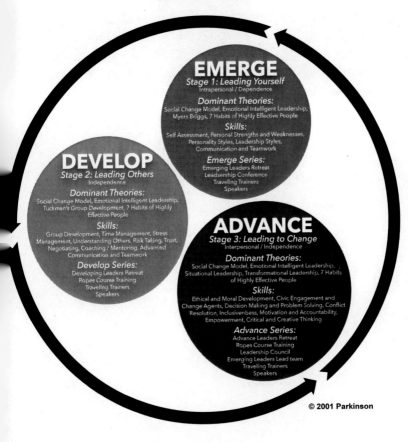

PARKINSON'S LEADER DEVELOPMENT MODEL

EMERGE
Stage 1: Leading Yourself
Intrapersonal / Dependence

Dominant Theories:
Social Change Model, Emotional Intelligent Leadership,
Myers Briggs, 7 Habits of Highly Effective People

Skills:
Self Assessment, Personal Strengths and Weaknesses,
Personality Styles, Leadership Styles,
Communication and Teamwork

Emerge Series:
Emerging Leaders Retreat
Leadership Conference
Traveling Trainers
Speakers

DEVELOP
Stage 2: Leading Others
Independence

Dominant Theories:
Social Change Model, Emotional Intelligent Leadership,
Tuckman's Group Development, 7 Habits of Highly
Effective People

Skills:
Group Development, Time Management, Stress
Management, Understanding Others, Risk Taking, Trust,
Negotiating, Coaching / Mentoring, Advanced
Communication and Teamwork

Develop Series:
Developing Leaders Retreat
Ropes Course Training
Traveling Trainers
Speakers

ADVANCE
Stage 3: Leading to Change
Interpersonal / Independence

Dominant Theories:
Social Change Model, Emotional Intelligent Leadership,
Situational Leadership, Transformational Leadership, 7 Habits
of Highly Effective People

Skills:
Ethical and Moral Development, Civic Engagement and
Change Agents, Decision Making and Problem Solving, Conflict
Resolution, Inclusivenbess, Motivation and Accountability,
Empowerment, Critical and Creative Thinking

Advance Series:
Advance Leaders Retreat
Ropes Course Training
Leadership Council
Emerging Leaders Lead team
Traveling Trainers
Speakers

© 2001 Parkinson

Series. A series is an intensive workshop or seminar that offers multiple sessions on a specific subject.

Conference. A conference is a one-day leadership summit that is open to all skill levels.

Workshop. A workshop is an educational seminar or series of meetings for a small group that emphasizes interaction and collaboration.

Speaker Program. A speaker program is a one-time trainer or keynote that students can participate in.

One can consider a speaker series.

Traveling Trainers. Traveling trainers bring the training to the group or team.

Service Learning Opportunities: or Skilled-Based Training. Skilled-based training is a developmental experience in which individuals gain knowledge and practice behaviors necessary to hone existing skills or develop new skills.

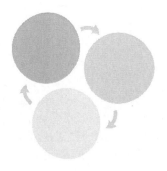

CHAPTER 8

PLDP Emerge: Leading Self

At the beginning of the program, it is important to provide the opportunity for students to explore both their strengths and areas in which they need to develop. What are they good at and what do they need to work on? As student's progress through the PLDP they will explore ways to capitalize on their strengths, while also identifying and improving upon their challenges.

Stage One: Emerge

The first stage of the PLDP, Emerge, is designed to help students develop self-awareness and self-confidence, along with an introduction to the basic leadership skills of communication and teamwork. Students must be capable of a certain degree of self-management and self-leadership before they are able to gain the trust of followers necessary to lead others. This is accomplished by providing programs that introduce self-assessment and allow students to explore their strengths and challenges, identify their personality type, and understand their preferred leadership styles.

You cannot lead others until you lead yourself. Leaders must understand who they are and believe in themselves.

They need to understand their strengths and challenges as well as personality and leadership styles. If they can't, it will be hard for them to understand where others are coming from and how they fit into the process.

In addition to developing self-awareness and self-confidence, stage one introduces two essential leadership skills: communication and teamwork. All of us can remember a team we worked with that had difficulty accomplishing its goal. Think about where the issue stemmed from. In all likelihood, there was a lack of effective communication and/or a failure to cooperate as a group. For this reason, the PLDP introduces communication and teamwork in the first stage and hones these skills throughout the rest of the program.

The Emerge stage draws from the following models, frameworks, and theories:

- The first three C's (Consciousness of Self, Congruence, & Commitment) of *The Social Change Model* developed by the Higher Education Research Institute

- "Consciousness of Self" in *Emotional Intelligent Leadership* by Dr. Marcy Shankman and Dr. Scott Allen

- Myers-Briggs Type Indicator by Katherine Cook Briggs and Isabel Briggs Myers

- Covey's first three habits (proactive, begin with the end in mind, and put first things first) from *7 Habits of Highly Effective People* by Stephen Covey

Additional Resources:

- *Strengthfinders 2.0* by Tom Rath

- *DISC Personality Test* by Corexcel

- McGregors XY Theory by Douglas McGregor

- True Colors Personality Test created by Don Lory

- *Multiple Intelligence* by Howard Gardner

Learning Outcomes

As a result of attending programs in the Emerge stage, students will develop the following skills and competencies.

Communication Skills:

- Being able to convey information and meaning

- Learning verbal and non-verbal communication

- Becoming an active listener

Basic Teamwork Skills:

- Recognizing that a team's output exceeds the sum of the individual

- Utilizing the strengths of all members of the group

- Acknowledging the weaknesses of members

- Developing a shared group agenda

- Building a consensual decision

Self-Awareness:

- Recognizing personal and leadership strengths and weaknesses

- Discovering their personality type and preferred leadership styles

- Developing personal values and beliefs

Self-Confidence:

- Increasing their self-efficacy and increasing personal discipline

• Gaining the confidence to lead others

Programming

There are several types of programs that can be used to accomplish the developmental goals of the Emerge Stage. These include, but are not limited to the following:

Emerge Series

The Emerge Series is a 4-6 week seminar that convenes for 2 hours each week and includes the completion of a three-hour community service activity. The main focus of this series is to explore "leading yourself." The curriculum includes self-assessment, team building, and training in effective communication. Sessions should be interactive and experiential to engage participants in order for them to get the most out of your training. Research has shown that experiential learning is the most effective method for delivering leadership programs. Faculty and staff from your campus, as well as external constituents such as alumni, professional colleagues, and business leaders are great resources to serve as guest speakers on relevant topics. Below is a sample outline for a 5-week series.

Sample Outline for Emerge Series

Week 1: Introductions/Icebreakers/Program Review/ Service Project Teams

Week 2: Communication

Week 3: Personality and/or Leadership Styles

Week 4: Understanding Strengths and Challenges

Week 5: Presentations/Recognition

Emerge Retreat

This retreat is a 2-night, 3-day program that is led by a team of experienced student leaders (Lead Team) who are selected through an application process. The retreat is designed to help students become more self-aware, self-confident, and begin learning basic leadership skills. Participants are nominated by coaches, advisors, staff, and/or faculty. All nominated students must submit an application. This retreat is based on 30 participants, but can be more or less depending on your budget.

Sample Outline for Emerge Retreat

Day 1

Name Game/Energizer: "Breaking the Ice" and getting the group to know each other is an important part of any retreat. Don't rush this process.

Dinner/Goals: Communicate what the goals are and allow participants to add to those goals.

Team Builder: Team building is one of the essential competencies in the Emerge Stage; spend time introducing the topic.

Defining a Leader: This session should provide the opportunity to explore the characteristics of effective leaders and develop their personal definition of leadership.

Free Time: This is the best part about retreat. It allows students to get to know each other and form life- long bonds. Keep this time unstructured, but offer opportunities to eat, play games, and dance to name few.

Day 2

Breakfast

Energizer: Wake everyone up! Get them ready for the day.

Rotating Session I: (Rotating sessions are a great way to break the larger group into three smaller groups, which in turn changes the learning process for students)

Leadership Styles: A competency in Emerge. Provide an opportunity for students to explore their personal leadership style, as well as, others. Begin to explore how to work with different styles.

Self-Assessment: A competency in Emerge. Administer a sefl-assessment exercise that allows students to explore their strengths and challenges.

Time Management: Offer tips and tricks for how to manage time.

Rotating Session II

Break

Lunch

Rotating Session III

Communication: Communication is a core competency within Emerge. Spend time educating participants on the importance of communication, effective communication, types of communication, and how to communicate

Break

Reaching Dependence: Explore Covey's first three habits.

Dinner

Board Breaking (or another activity that focuses on Self-Awareness/Self-Confidence): Board Breaking is a power seminar that challenges students to see that they can do anything that they put their mind to. This session should cover mentorship, developing a support network, and, most importantly, believing in oneself.

Free Time

Day 3

Breakfast

Energizer

Bringing it Home: It is crucial that you take the time to tie what was learned throughout the weekend to "real" life. How can this be applied to my club, organization, etc.?

Closing: Take the time to close out your retreat. People need closure. This should be reflective and positive.

Theory to Practice

There are many ways to put theory to practice. You are already doing it. Now you have to connect the dots and be more intentional with bringing the two together. Remember, your programming should be creative, interactive, and educational. Students don't want a lecture on theory. Create programs that bring the theory to life and as you deliver your programs, mention the theory that supports the topic. Below is a quick sampling of ways in which you can connect the theory to the practice:

1. Utilize the first 3 C's of the Social Change Model
   - Engage in self-assessment
   - Explore commitment

2. Create a session using the Myers-Briggs Type Indicator
   - Explore personality types

3. Introduce a Values Clarification workshop

4. Identify Leadership Styles

5. Emotional Intelligent Leadership: Consciousness of Self

6. Explore Honest Self Understanding

7. Provide the environment for dialogue around "self"

8. Explore Covey's first three habits

9. Offer a workshop on visioning

Emerge is a crucial piece to the PLDP, which provides the foundation for a student's development. Strong leaders are confident and have a sense of self-awareness. This part of the training is important and should not be rushed. Do your best to make sure students have met the learning objectives in this stage before moving to the next, which is Develop.

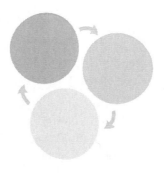

CHAPTER 9

PLDP Develop: Leading Others

A developing leader is defined as an individual who has a foundation of leadership outlined in the Emerge Stage. This person may be someone who has held or is holding a leadership role within their club, organization or team and has completed the basic leadership training provided in the prior Stage.

Stage 2: Develop

Influencing towards change is best accomplished through collaboration and teamwork. Knowing the accompanying skills of working in groups and teams assists the leader in advancing through Stage 2. Specific skills within this stage include: dealing with differing ideas, delegating tasks fairly, and empowering others. Leaders should learn how to work with others by sharing ideas, bridging differences in communication styles, reinforcing the contributions of all members, and motivating one another.

In stage 2, students learn about group development and teamwork. This stage is designed to teach students how to work with others and collaborate with different leadership styles and varying personality types. The programming encourages participants to bring their own views to the table while appreciating other's perspective.

In addition, Develop focuses on leading others by learning how to work with their specific strengths and challenges. The central question becomes, "how can one leader compliment another leader?" Because one team member's strength will be another's challenge, programs in the Develop Stage begin to teach students relationship and team-building skills of trust, coaching, mentoring, and risk taking. Develop teaches students to see that all team members bring value to their groups.

The Develop stage draws from the following models, frameworks, and theories:

- The second set of C's (Collaboration, Common Purpose, & Controversy with Civility) within the *Social Change Model* by the Higher Education Institute for Research

- Tuckman's Group Development by Bruce Tuckman

- "Consciousness of Others" in *Emotional Intelligent Leadership* by Marcy Shankmen and Scott Allen

- Covey's next three habits (think win/win, seek to understand, then to be understood, and create synergy) on independence in *7 Habits of Highly Effective People* by Stephen Covey

Learning Outcomes

As a result of attending programs in the Develop Stage, students will develop the following skills and competencies.

Teamwork Skills:

- Recognizing that a team's output exceeds what can be accomplished by separate individuals

- Utilizing the strengths of all members of the group

- Acknowledging the weaknesses of members and finding ways to overcome these weaknesses

- Developing a shared group agenda

- Building a consensual decision

Trust:

- Learning the importance of trust and recognizing the need for honesty and truthfulness in all team interactions

- Building confidence in another individual's intentions and motives when honorable

- Aligning actions with words in order to make each individual a trusted team member

Risk Taking:

- Being able to challenge themselves

- Having the ability to attempt the unknown

- Inclusiveness

- Embracing a more diverse view

- Moving from discussion (exploring a topic) to dialogue (building consensus and solving problems)

- Defining and appreciating diversity

- Working with others who are different from yourself

Programming

Programs that have been developed to assist with this leadership development in this stage include, but are not limited to:

The Develop Series

The Develop Series is a 4-6 week seminar that convenes for two hours per week. The main focus of this series is to develop skills associated with collaboration and teamwork. The curriculum includes leading others, trust, coaching, and advanced communication. In addition the participants are required to complete a group community service activity.

Sample Outline for Develop Series

Week 1: Introductions/Program Review/Team Builder

Week 2: Interpersonal Communication

Week 3: Trust and Risk Taking

Week 4: Coaching & Mentoring

Week 5: Closing/Recognition

Develop Retreat

This program is designed to provide students the opportunity to master the skill of working with others. The best way to describe this experience is a mix between Survivor and Amazing Race. The retreat is built around Bruce Tuckman's five stages for group development.

This experience is designed for a small group of developing leaders. The leaders are nominated and then complete an application process. From the pool of applicants, 20 participants are chosen and divided into 4 teams of 5. The retreat consists of 5 main challenges, with the option to include up to 5 bonus challenges. The challenges should test students mentally, emotionally, and physically. Throughout the retreat, teams play for food, shelter, showers, and points in each of the challenges. By the end of the retreat, students should have learned the 5 stages of group development and improved in the areas of teamwork, communication, problem solving, and decision making.

Sample Outline of the Develop Retreat: Extreme Challenge

Day 1

Bonus Challenge #1 - Team Flag: Provide each team with a wooden rod, white sheet, and markers. Teams must create a flag that represents their team color and name. Most creative flag receives the bonus points.

Leave Campus

Challenge #1 - Riddle: Create or find a riddle that is extremely challenging.

Arrive at your destination

Challenge #2 - Extreme Challenge (A team race): Set up a series of challenges that are physical and mental in nature. Utilize the entire camp, campus or venue.

Set up camp, eat dinner, and process: Based on the points they have earned from the previous challenges, each team will receive their assigned shelter and food. It is up to the teams to create their own experience for the rest of the evening.

Bonus Challenge #2 - Questions for "Exploring Leadership": This can be implemented anywhere in the program. Test the teams on their knowledge of Tuckman's Group Development. This should be delivered as a competition or game. Make it fun.

Day 2:

Bonus Challenge #3 - Song and Dance: Optional, provide a clue for the teams to meet up, once convened each team will be given fifteen minutes to prepare a song and dance, performance is judged on creativity and enthusiasm.

Breakfast (based on your place in the competition): Food is assigned by what place you currently hold.

Mind Over Matter: This should be an extreme mental challenge. Provide an activity(s) that forces the team to think outside the box and problem solve.

Break

Bonus Challenge #4 - Word Search

Challenge #4 - Build and Race a Go-Cart: Provide a team activity that is hands on and requires students to problem solve, make decisions, communicate, trust, etc.

Food is provided based on what place you hold in the competition.

Challenge #5 - Scavenger Hunt: This is a physical and mental challenge. Use the entire camp, campus, or venue. Provide a set of clues that takes the team from one location to the next. Again, this needs to be hard. If you want to make it more extreme, add some challenges at some of the stopping points.

Bringing it together: Debrief, process, discuss the stages of group development.

Group dinner

Theory to Practice

1. Utilize the second 3 C's of the Social Change Model
   - Offer team building exercises

2. Emotional Intelligent Leadership: Consciousness of Others
   - Explore the power of influence
   - Create a workshop on coaching

3. Tuckman's Group Development
   - Build an experience that provides the opportunity for students to go through the stages of development

4. Explore Covey's second three habits
   - Introduce a workshop on communication
   - Review diversity and inclusiveness, open to new ideas

As students progress through this program, they become more aware of themselves and others. Once they have developed this firm sense of self-identity and are actively skill building, it becomes time to provide participants with opportunities to put those skills to practice, while learning more advanced skill sets. The Advance Stage should be the ultimate goal of your program. This is the point in which "true leadership" takes place. Together, let's explore the third stage, which is Advance.

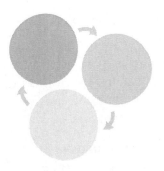

CHAPTER 10

PLDP Advance: Leading Change

An advanced leader is defined as someone who has an extensive leadership background. This person may be someone who has held or is holding a leadership position and has completed several leadership programs. The programs in stage three are for students who want to fine tune their current leadership skills and to effectively put their skills into practice.

Stage 3: Advance

The ultimate goal of any leadership development program should be to produce individuals who are prepared to contribute to society. Whether in their local community, place of work, or in pursuit of a particular cause, leaders who graduate or complete leadership programs should be able to understand what it takes to lead societal change. The Advance Stage focuses on leading to change and living in an interdependent world. This requires putting previously learned skills into practice. It also includes the development of higher-level leadership skills, challenging students to delegate roles and empower and motivate the other members of their team. Given the influence advance leaders will have on those around them, this stage puts particular emphasis on the importance of making ethical decisions.

Skills to develop or strengthen in the Advance Stage include: ethical and moral development, decision making, problem solving, conflict resolution, inclusiveness, motivation, accountability, delegation, and empowerment.

The Advance stage draws from the following models, frameworks, and theories:

- Citizenship and Change: *Social Change Model* by The Higher Education Institute for Research

- Situational Leadership II by Ken Blanchard

- Transformation Leadership by James MacGregor Burns

- "Consciousness of Context" in *Emotional Intelligent Leadership* by Marcy Shankman and Scott Allen

- The 7th Habit (sharpening the saw) in *7 Habits of Highly Effective People* by Stephen Covey

Additional Resources:

- Servant Leadership by Richard Greenleaf

- *The Leadership Challenge* by James Kouzes and Barry Posner

Learning Outcomes

- As a result of attending programs in the Advance Stage, students will develop the following skills and competencies.

Creative Thinking Skills:

- Brainstorming new and innovative ideas

- Developing new paradigms to overcome challenges

Decision Making Skills:

- Being able to make and defend a decision based on sound reasoning

- Determining when to make a team decision or when to seek outside consultation

- Exploring the leadership roles in group decision making

- Focusing on tasks in order of importance

- Seeking opinions from team members with an openness to other perspectives

Problem Solving and Critical Thinking Skills:

- Identifying a problem and being able to offer different solutions

- Learning how to solve problems by developing a strategy

- Developing the ability to think on your feet

Conflict Resolution Skills:

- Learning how to identify problems

- Providing constructive feedback for personal change

- Confronting others with problems and concerns and listening attentively to their response

- Accepting constructive feedback from others

- Applying the various conflict resolution styles to different situations

Delegation and Empowerment Skills:

- Learning that you are only as good as your team

- Assigning responsibility for accomplishing objectives

- Learning to delegate effectively and prioritizing tasks

Coaching Skills:

- Enabling others to contribute more fully and productively

- Creating a partnership for achieving results

- Collaborating with others to pursue goals more efficiently and effectively

Students Ability to Create a Vision:

- Create a vision and build commitment among team members

- Learning the practical skills needed to implement that vision

- Seeing yourself as an agent of change

Group Development/Motivation:

- Creating synergy in a group

- Learning the stages of group development and how to advance through them

- Keeping the team on task

- Becoming a visionary leader

- Learning what motivates your team members

- Raising the motivation level through various recognition techniques

Students Ability to Create Change:

- Being able to identify a problem on campus or in the community and create a leadership project that creates change

Programming

Programs for the Advance Stage include, but are not limited to, the following:

Advance Series

The Advance Series is a 4-6 week program that is designed to teach advanced skills through participation in an extended service project. The participants are divided into teams of 3-5 members. They are assigned a topic (e.g. problem solving, decision making, conflict resolution) and each team is charged with choosing a service project of their choice. While completing the service project, the team is also doing research on their assigned topic. At the end of the program, the teams are asked to present their service project and, based on their research and field experience, to provide training on their topic to participants from the other groups.

Sample Outline for Advance Series

Week 1: Introductions/Break into small teams/Assign Topic and Service Project

Week 2: Begin working on the service project and researching assigned topic

Week 3: As students continue their work, check in with each team and offer any needed support

Week 4: Complete service project and research and begin working on the training presentation

Week 5: Participants offer training on their assigned topic and present their service project to the larger group; after all groups have presented, hold a closing ceremony recognizing the contributions of all participants

Advance Experience

The Advance Experience is a 4 night, 5 day service learning leadership program. This program is geared towards advanced leaders and uses the Situational Leadership II model. It is designed for a small group of leaders (no more than ten) and seeks to combine service and leadership. The students spend five days serving in the local community, while also learning applicable leadership skills through workshops and practical experiences. They sleep, eat, work, and learn within this community. Each day ends with intentional reflection about how situational leadership was put to practice.

Check with your local YMCA or community centers for shelter. Projects vary from painting, handy man work, serving at food pantries or soup kitchens, or working with kids. There are no limits to what projects you choose, just keep in mind that you should be choosing based on the need of your community, rather than what you want. To achieve true service learning, establish community partnerships and make sure reciprocity is present. Additionally, be sure that the participants always end each day with intentional reflection on the work they have done. The literature on service learning clearly shows the need for both reciprocity and reflection for authentic service learning.

Sample Outline for Advance Experience

Day 1

Convene

Head to the community center

- Settle in to assigned space, team lunch

Opening Presentation: "What is Service Learning?"

Service Project I (could be something at the shelter

that you are staying at)

Presentations: Have pairs of students present their research on the community that they will be serving; presentations should focus on demographics, and social, economic, and political issues)

Presentation I: Leadership Theory

Dinner

Group Activities: Team building, social activities

Day 2

Community Breakfast (made by the participants)

Service Project II

Lunch

Service Project III

Reflection

Community Dinner (made by the participants)

Group Social (e.g. mini golf)

Day 3

Community Breakfast

Service Project IV

Lunch (eat in the community you are serving in)

Service Project V

Presentation II: Mentoring

Community Dinner

Reflection

Group Social

Day 4

Community Breakfast

Presentation III: Team Activity

Bringing it together

Closing lunch at a local restaurant

Return to your institution

Theory to Practice

1. Utilize the final "C" of the Social Change Model

   - Create an service project that allows students put their skills to practice

2. Emotional Intelligent Leadership: Consciousness of Context

   - Challenge students to be aware of their environment

3. Introduce Situational Leadership II

   - Practice Situational Leadership through a team project

4. Explore Covey's seventh habit

   - Provide a capstone program that incorporates all leadership skills and competencies

The PLDP incorporates additional programs and experiences that can be utilized anywhere within your program. These include the Leadership Council, Leadership Conference, and Traveling Trainers.

PLDP: Additional Programs

Leadership Council

This team of students is a group of advanced leaders who

create, organize, and implement the entire leadership program. This team includes 7-9 members who are selected through an application process and are "the best of the best" among the leaders on campus. These students should have successfully completed a majority of the offerings in your leadership program and have a high level of skill and competency. The leadership council is a capstone for the leadership program and provides an opportunity to put learned skills into practice. This team is supported by a professional staff member who is assigned to developing leadership programs on their campus. Participants should be chosen through a nomination and application process. They are responsible for creating and implementing the entire leadership program on your campus. Involving students in the development and delivery of your programs can make a tremendous impact on individual and program success.

Leadership Conference

Most institutions offer a one-day leadership conference for their students. Your conference can cover all three stages in the PLDP.

Sample Outline for the Leadership Conference

Registration

Welcome
- Remarks from the University President

Education Session Block I
- Self-assessment (Emerge)
- Communication (Develop)
- Problem solving and decision making (Advance)
- Citizenship (Advance)

Education Session Block II
- Active Listening (Emerge)

- Creative Leadership (Develop)
- Empowering Others (Advance)
- Crisis Management (Advance)

Keynote Luncheon

Education Session Block III

- Bucket List to Becoming a Great Leader (Emerge)
- Mentor-ship/Coaching (Develop)
- Ethical Leadership (Advance)

Team Challenge (provide an activity that engages all participants)

Closing Remarks

Traveling Trainers

Are your athletes too busy to attend a leadership series? Do you have trouble getting resident students out of their hall? You are not alone! This program is a great way to bring the training to the students.

The traveling trainer program provides your organizations, teams, and/or classes the opportunity to enhance their leadership skills and competencies by bringing the training to them.

Teams already have their practice time. Clubs and organizations have their meeting times and classes are scheduled. Why not take advantage of this time and bring the training to them?

This program is run through the leadership council. Each council member develops a canned session on topics like communication, teamwork, time management, etc. The program is then marketed to coaches, clubs presidents and advisors, and faculty. The intent is to encourage clients to contact the council for training.

For example, if an organization president contacts the traveling trainer coordinator for a session on communication, the coordinator would send the information to the council member who offers the communication workshop. It would then be up to this council member to reach out to the organization president to set up the training. If the trainer cannot do the program (based on a scheduling conflict), it should be delegated to another council member.

What is great about this program is that we are bringing the training to our students, but it also provides advanced leaders the opportunity to create a leadership session (which will develop their mastery of the subject) and work on their presentation skills.

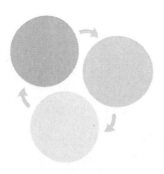

CHAPTER 11

Assessing Your Efforts

According to Beltyukova and Fox (2002), student satisfaction is an "ever-present campus variable, a key outcome of higher education and a quality enhancement tool design to improve the quality of the student experience" (p. 161). They believe that colleges and universities use student satisfaction data to improve and change campus environments, therefore adding to the overall development of students. However, measuring the effectiveness of anything is not an easy task. Upcraft and Shuh (1996) believe that "satisfaction needs to be framed by the institution's mission and the mission and goals of the various programs, services, and learning opportunities that are part of the assessment" (p. 163).

Chambers (1992) is concerned that people simply are not doing this. They are failing to evaluate programs to prove that they do contribute to the students' overall development. He continues by stating that "it is important to acquire information about leadership programs to make decisions about the process employed in their implementation" (p. 340).

How do we do that? Unfortunately it is not as easy to assess a leadership program, but we must try. Assessment is an important aspect of what we do and it is even more important to provide evidence that our programs are making a difference, especially in a time when Higher Education is being held accountable for "value added." This chapter includes a comprehensive assessment tool that compliments the Parkinson's Leadership Development Program (PLDP).

The assessment tool was developed over several years through a formative and summative process. It reflects the three stages of the PLDP, along with the learning outcomes identified in Chapter 6. The questions in the assessment tool were developed through field experience and the current literature on leadership theory and practice. To refine the original draft of the assessment, it was submitted to a formative committee for review. The committee consisted of practitioners who were involved with leadership programs on their campus. Based on the feedback of this group, the assessment was revised and the updated draft was sent to a summative committee comprised of experts in the field of leadership development. Upon their review, further revisions were made, and the effectiveness of the assessment was strengthened. The final assessment tool can be found in this chapter.

The questions in this tool use a Likert scale in which a question is posed and the person completing the survey is asked to choose one of four responses: strongly disagree, disagree, agree, or strongly agree. The assessment consists of 85 questions and focuses on the learning outcomes discussed in the above chapters.

The tool can be used in two ways. It was initially developed to be used as a post assessment for each stage in the PLDP. Used in this way, the assessment helped the staff and leadership council to judge whether a student leader was ready to move to the next stage.

The second way the tool can be used is to give students the entire survey before they begin your leadership program and again at the completion of your program. By using the assessment in this way, it is possible to evaluate the overall impact of the leadership program as a whole, based on the reported change of those students who have participated in all three stages. The goal is to measure the growth that the student may or may not have gained after completing your comprehensive leadership program.

The limitation of this tool (present in all forms of self-assessment) is that the students are self-reporting and, typically, people tend to score themselves higher than they actually are. Keep this in mind when reviewing the results. Also, when you administer the assessment, encourage the participants to answer all questions as honestly as possible, reminding them of the important role that self-awareness plays in their growth as leaders.

PLDP Assessment Tool:
© Parkinson 2003

Instructions: For each of the following statements, choose the response that most accurately reflects your current attitude, belief, or behavior, using the scale provided (1 = Strongly Disagree, 2 = Disagree, 3 = Agree, and 4 = Strongly Agree).

Stage I	SD	D	A	SA
1. Problems with the team are the responsibility of all members.	1	2	3	4
2. I know and can explain to others what my personal definition of leadership is.	1	2	3	4
3. I encourage others to talk by showing interest, smiling, nodding, and using other positive body language.	1	2	3	4
4. It is easy for me to praise others.	1	2	3	4

	SD	D	A	SA
5. I have an "all in it together" attitude when working with others.	1	2	3	4
6. I am self-confident in my social skills.	1	2	3	4
7. I am a team player and enjoy working with others more than I enjoy working alone.	1	2	3	4
8. I feel confident in leading followers.	1	2	3	4
9. I am a well-organized person.	1	2	3	4
10. I have high self-esteem.	1	2	3	4
11. I welcome the opportunity to speak in front of a group.	1	2	3	4
12. I am able to identify my strengths as a leader.	1	2	3	4
13. When I think others are missing information or contradicting themselves, I ask direct questions to get them to explain their point of view more fully.	1	2	3	4
14. I am confident that I can take charge of a group.	1	2	3	4

	SD	D	A	SA
15. I am confident in the quality of my writing skills.	1	2	3	4
16. I am able to delegate roles and responsibilities in a group.	1	2	3	4
17. When working in a group, I am able to identify my leadership style.	1	2	3	4
18. When working in a group, I develop a shared agenda.	1	2	3	4
19. I feel confident in my abilities as a leader.	1	2	3	4
20. When I don't understand something, I let the speaker know and ask for further clarification.	1	2	3	4

Stage II

	SD	D	A	SA
21. I am able to work with others who have different styles than me.	1	2	3	4
22. I enjoy work that involves abstract thinking.	1	2	3	4
23. Some of my best ideas have come from building on the ideas of others.	1	2	3	4

	SD	D	A	SA
24. I am honest with my team members.	1	2	3	4
25. I explore how differences might be utilized as assets in a team project.	1	2	3	4
26. I am able to make my behavior consistent with my intentions and values by practicing what I preach.	1	2	3	4
27. I would not steal from the organization.	1	2	3	4
28. I act as an ally for people who are different from other members of the group.	1	2	3	4
29. I work to instill confidence in others.	1	2	3	4
30. I challenge myself and reflect critically on decisions I make.	1	2	3	4
31. Playing with a new idea is fun, even if it does not benefit me in the end.	1	2	3	4
32. I am not afraid to commit to and take purposeful risks.	1	2	3	4
33. I take risks even when I am not supported by others.	1	2	3	4

	SD	D	A	SA
34. When I am working on a task, I work by the motto "slow and steady."	1	2	3	4
35. I volunteer to share ideas and resources with people in other groups.	1	2	3	4
36. I am always searching for a way to improve things.	1	2	3	4
37. I like to try new things.	1	2	3	4
38. I feel my teammates trust me when I work in groups.	1	2	3	4
39. I embrace people who are different from me.	1	2	3	4
40. I help team members understand their own feelings and attitudes about people who are different.	1	2	3	4

Stage III

	SD	D	A	SA
41. In a complex situation, I do not make a decision alone.	1	2	3	4
42. I have the ability to imagine different and better conditions and ways to achieve them.	1	2	3	4

	SD	D	A	SA
43. I am able to offer a compelling vision for where a group needs to go.	1	2	3	4
44. When delegating a task I establish check points and milestones to obtain feedback and provide support.	1	2	3	4
45. When leading I have the ability to establish systemic change.	1	2	3	4
46. When solving a problem I take a positive approach throughout the entire process.	1	2	3	4
47. I generously praise people who help me get work accomplished.	1	2	3	4
48. I permit the group to make the decision within prescribed limits.	1	2	3	4
49. I have the ability to spot opportunities that other people may overlook.	1	2	3	4
50. When the group's work is completed I celebrate the accomplishments of the team.	1	2	3	4

	SD	D	A	SA
51. I can visualize how a solution to a problem might look, sound, taste, feel, and smell.	1	2	3	4
52. I provide modeling and training.	1	2	3	4
53. Before confronting a team member, I identify the problem and possible solutions.	1	2	3	4
54. I ask the other person what he or she is hoping to achieve in the situation.	1	2	3	4
55. To avoid conflict, I put the concerns of others ahead of my own.	1	2	3	4
56. I focus on the task and keep any negative personal feelings in check.	1	2	3	4
57. In a confrontation I like to create a win-win situation.	1	2	3	4
58. I am able to design a plan that will help carry out change.	1	2	3	4
59. I am able to delegate tasks and assign responsibility.	1	2	3	4

	SD	D	A	SA
60. In order to create change, I initiate strategies that followers agree upon.	1	2	3	4
61. I am able to identify a problem and offer several possible solutions.	1	2	3	4
62. I assign the right duties to the right people.	1	2	3	4
63. I can think on my feet during difficult situations.	1	2	3	4
64. In trying to solve a problem, I present the problem to the group members in a meeting, gather suggestions, and then make a decision based on their input.	1	2	3	4
65. I develop a supportive working relationship among my teammates.	1	2	3	4
66. When confronting others, I try to reach consensus with the second party.	1	2	3	4
67. I collaborate with others to improve results.	1	2	3	4
68. I give constant feedback to avoid confusion within a group.	1	2	3	4

	SD	D	A	SA
69. I can create commitment in others through communicating a compelling vision.	1	2	3	4
70. I have the ability to articulate and imagine a vision of a future that is significantly better than the present.	1	2	3	4
71. I am able to positively influence the behavior of others when pursuing a certain outcome.	1	2	3	4
72. I explain exactly what I expect to the person I'm trying to motivate.	1	2	3	4
73. When feasible, I delegate responsibilities rather than tasks.	1	2	3	4
74. I am able to create synergy and cohesiveness in a group.	1	2	3	4
75. I challenge the group to perform with high levels of commitment and competence.	1	2	3	4
76. I present the problem, and facilitate the solution, by defining the problem to be solved and the boundaries in which the decision must be made.	1	2	3	4

	SD	D	A	SA
77. I delegate to empower my team members.	1	2	3	4
78. I am able to influence others to achieve organizational objectives.	1	2	3	4
79. I never blame or embarrass my teammates.	1	2	3	4
80. When bringing a group together for the first time, I provide the opportunity for everyone to get to know each other.	1	2	3	4
81. I inspire people with a vision of a better future that is sufficiently attractive to convince them that the old approaches are no longer adequate.	1	2	3	4
82. When somebody performs well, I recognize his or her accomplishments.	1	2	3	4
83. When confronting others I listen carefully and attentively to what they have to say in response.	1	2	3	4
84. I have the ability to communicate complex ideas and goals in a clear, compelling way.	1	2	3	4

	SD	D	A	SA
85. I understand that groups go through stages of development.	1	2	3	4

*Questions adapted from:

Dubrin, A. J. (2004). *Leadership: Research findings, practice, and skills.* New York: Houghton Mifflin.

Lussier, N. R., & Achua, F. C. (2001). *Leadership: Theory, application, skill development.* Cincinnati, OH: South Western College.

Scoring

Questions 1-20 assess the skills and competencies for Stage 1. The highest possible overall score is an 80, and the lowest is a 20. A score between 0-49 indicates that the student *has not learned the skills and competencies* of Stage 1; a score between 50-69 indicates that the student *has learned some of the skills and competencies* of Stage 1; and a score between 70-80 indicates the student *has learned most of the skills and competencies* for Stage 1. In addition to the overall score, each of the four focus areas of stage 1, self-awareness, self-confidence, communication, and teamwork, can be looked at individually.

Put the appropriate score next to the corresponding question number. Add each individual skill set. Then add all four skill sets together to get your total score.

Self-Awareness

2. _____

9. _____

12. _____

Self-Confidence

4. _____

6. _____

8. _____

14. _____   10. _____

17. _____   19. _____

Total: _____   **Total:** _____

Communication   *Teamwork*

3. _____   1. _____

11. _____   5. _____

13. _____   7. _____

15. _____   16. _____

20. _____   18. _____

Total: _____   **Total:** _____

Total Score for Stage I: _____

Questions 21-40 assess the skills and competencies for Stage 2. The highest possible overall score is an 80, and the lowest is a 20. A score between 0-49 indicates that the student *has not learned the skills and competencies* of Stage 2; a score between 50-69 indicates that the student *has learned some of the skills and competencies* of Stage 2; and a score between 70-80 indicates the student *has learned most of the skills and competencies* for Stage 2. In addition to the overall score, each of the four focus areas of Stage 2, creative thinking, trust, risk, and inclusiveness, can be looked at individually.

Put the appropriate score next to the corresponding question number. Add each individual skill set. Then add all four skill sets together to get your total score.

Creative Thinking

22. _____

23. _____

31. _____

34. _____

36. _____

Total: _____

Trust

24. _____

26. _____

27. _____

29. _____

38. _____

Total: _____

Risk

30. _____

32. _____

33. _____

35. _____

37. _____

Total: _____

Inclusiveness

21. _____

25. _____

28. _____

39. _____

40. _____

Total: _____

Total Score for Stage II: _____

Questions 41-85 assess the mastery of the skills and competencies for Stage 3. The highest possible overall score is a 180, and the lowest possible score is a 45. A score between 0-134 indicates that the student *has not learned the skills and competencies* for Stage 3; a score between 135-169 indicates that the student *has learned some of the skills and competencies* for Stage 3; and a score between 170-180 indicates that the student *has learned most of the skills and competencies* for Stage 3. The nine focus areas of Stage 3 are decision making, problem solving and critical thinking, conflict resolution, delegation, coaching, vision, motivation, group development, and change. In addition to the overall score, each of the nine focus areas of Stage 3 can be looked at individually.

Put the appropriate score next to the corresponding question number. Add each individual skill sets. Then add all four skill sets together to get your total score.

Decision Making	*Problem Solving & Critical Thinking*	*Conflict Resolution*
41. _____	46. _____	53. _____
48. _____	49. _____	55. _____
56. _____	51. _____	57. _____
64. _____	61. _____	66. _____
76. _____	63. _____	83. _____
Total: _____	**Total:** _____	**Total:** _____

Delegation	*Coaching*	*Vision*
44. _____	52. _____	42. _____
59. _____	65. _____	43. _____
62. _____	67. _____	69. _____
73. _____	68. _____	70. _____

77. _____	79. _____	84. _____
Total: _____	**Total:** _____	**Total:** _____

Motivation	*Group Development*	*Change*
47. _____	50. _____	45. _____
54. _____	74. _____	58. _____
71. _____	75. _____	60. _____
72. _____	80. _____	78. _____
82. _____	85. _____	81. _____
Total: _____	**Total:** _____	**Total:** _____

Total Score for Stage III: _____

Overall Total for Stages 1, 2, and 3: _____

Has Not Learned the Skills and Competencies in the Leadership Program = 0–85

Has Learned Some of the Skills and Competencies in the Leadership Program = 86–255

Has Learned Most of the Skills and Competences in the Leadership Program = 256–340

CHAPTER 12

The Freedom to Create

The PLDP presented in the previous chapters is actually an updated version of the original. It is important to point out that our work in leadership development should always be evolving. It is equally as important to share best practices with our colleagues and learn from each other.

For example, the PLDP reflects minor changes due to conversations with Rich Hurley, who has continued to build the leadership program at Bryant University. It is important to remember that change is necessary to achieve the highest levels of success in your leadership program.

There is no one way of delivering your leadership programs. As I outlined in Chapter 2, it is critical to look at best practices and create a program that works for your campus. Once you develop and implement your program, challenge yourself to re-evaluate frequently, and don't be afraid to make changes when needed.

Next Steps

Where do you go from here? It is recommended that you engage students, faculty, and staff in a strategic planning process. The first step in developing your plan is to identify your **Core Values**. Your core values are "how you spend your time." What is most important to you and your institution? What do you value most? After identifying your core values you can begin to create a vision for your program.

Your **Vision** is about "being." What do you want this leadership program to be? Where do you see yourself three years from now? How about five years from now? What do you want to be known for in the future? Once you have a good grasp on your vision, you can begin to work on your mission.

Your **Mission** is about "doing." What do you do on a day-to-day basis? How will you achieve your vision? Your mission statement should be concise, clear, direct, and pithy. You want people to be able to relate to and remember your mission.

When you believe you have your vision and mission set you can begin to identify and set your **Learning Outcomes** (see Chapter 5). These are the skills and competencies that you want your participants (students) to learn. The learning outcomes you choose should support your overall vision and the mission for the leadership program.

Once you create your learning outcomes, you are ready to set goals and action steps. The program **Goals** should support your core values, mission, vision, and learning outcomes. These are what you want to achieve in that given semester and/or year. They should be attainable, realistic, concise, and reasonable. Your **Action Steps** are the day-to-day tasks that help you move towards accomplishing your goals. They must be easy to identify and consist of visible steps that put your plan into action. These should be time sensitive, assigned to capable individuals, and measurable.

As you take in the content in this book and look at your blank canvas, know that you are not alone. This can be a very overwhelming process, but with the resources provided in this book, it doesn't have to be. Let this book be the first stroke in the leadership program you hope to create. Perhaps this will motivate you and give you the foundation that you were looking for. Keep on creating your works of art and never give up on your vision.

ABOUT THE AUTHOR

Dr. Hank Parkinson has 16 years of progressive experience in higher education administration and is an expert leadership trainer. He has worked at multiple institutions and is experienced in Student Activities, Operations, Orientation, First-year Experience, Leadership Development, Volunteerism, Greek Life, Residence Life, Multi-Cultural Affairs, and Recreation Services. Currently, he is the Associate Dean for Student Development and Residence Life at Fitchburg State University. His research interests include First-year Experience, Leadership Development, and Student Development.

Through his LTE Consulting, Hank trains student leaders and staff throughout the New England area and specializes in self-assessment, team building, organization development, and strategic planning. One of his most exhilarating seminars is Board Breaking, a training program which provides leaders with the opportunity to build self-confidence and self-awareness, all while stressing the importance of having a support net and a mentor.

To complement his training, Hank consults with institutions seeking to develop a strategic plan for their offices. As part of his doctorate work, he developed a comprehensive three-stage leadership development program that can be implemented on other campuses.

Hank believes that anyone can learn how to be leader with some training and practice. He is passionate about student development and believes that it is the responsibility of higher education to invest in a student's growth and development.

BIBLIOGRAPHY

Antoniadis J., Cianciolo T. A., & Sternberg J. R. (2004). *The nature of leadership*. London: Sage.

Amirianzedeh, M. Jaafari, P. Ghourchain, N., & Jowkar, B. (2010). College student leadership competencies development: A model. *International Journal for Cross-Disciplinary Subjects in Education*, 1(3).

Avolio J. Bruce, Walumbwa O. Fred, Weber J. Todd (2009). Leadership: Current theories, research, and future directions. *The Annual Review of Psychology, 60*, 421-49.

Beltyukova, S. A., & Fox, C. M. (2002). Student satisfaction as a measure of student development: Towards a universal metric. *NASPA Journal, 43*(2), 161-172.

Blanchard K., Zigarmi P., Zigarmi D. (2013). *Leadership and the One Minute Manager: Increasing Effectiveness Through Situational Leadership II*. New Your, NY, Harper Collins Publishers.

Blank, W. (2001). *The 108 skills of natural born leaders*. New York: American Management Association.

Boatman, S. A. (1999). The leadership audit: A process to enhance the development of student leadership. *NASPA Journal, 37*, 325-336.

Bogdan, R. C., & Biklen, S. K. (1998). *Qualitative research for education: An introduction to theory and methods*. Boston: Allyn & Bacon.

Bowling Green State University, Office of Campus Involvement (2003). *Office of Campus Involvement: Leadership development programs*. Retrieved October 20, 2003, from http://www.bgsu.edu

Brach, S. (2000, January 2). Leading the way: Colleges recognize growing need to offer leadership programs. *Chicago Tribune*, p. 3.

Buckner, K. J., & Williams, L. M. (1995, November). *Reconceptualizing university student leadership development programs: Applying the competing values model.* Paper presented at the annual meeting of the Speech Communication Association, San Antonio, TX.

Burns, B. S. (1995). Leadership studies: A new partnership between academic departments and student affairs. *NASPA Journal, 32,* 242-250.

Cacioppe, R. (1998). An integrated model and approach for the design of effective leadership development programs. *Leadership and Organization Development Journal, 19*(1), 44-53.

Chambers, R. (1992). The development of criteria to evaluate college student leadership programs: A delphi approach. *Journal of College Student Development, 33,* 339-347.

Council for the Advancement of Standards in Higher Education (2006). Guide for student leadership programs. Washington, D.C.

Clark, E. K., & Clark, B. M. (1999). *Choosing to lead.* Greensboro, NC: Center for Creative Leadership.

Covey, S. R., (1989). *The 7 Habits of Highly Effective People.* New York, NY: Simon & Schuster.

Cress, M. C., Astin, S. H., Zimmerman-Oster, K., & Burkhardt, C. J. (2001). Developmental outcomes of college students' involvement in leadership activities. *Journal of College Student Development, 42,* 15-27.

Day, V. D. (2001). Leadership development: A review in context. *Leadership Quarterly, 11,* 581-613.

Denney, N.H., (2013). *Zing! 21 Insights on Maximizing Your Influence.* Marion, MA: Zing! Publishing.

Denzin, N. K., & Lincoln, Y. S. (1994). *Handbook of qualitative research.* Thousands Oaks, CA: Sage.

Dubrin, A. J. (2004). *Leadership: Research findings, practice, and skills.* New York: Houghton Mifflin.

Dugan, J.P., Bohle, C.W., Gebhardt, M., Hofert, M., Wilk, E., & Cooney, M.A. (2011).

Influences of leadership program participation on students' capacities for socially responsible leadership. *Journal of Student Affairs Research and Practice. 48*(1), 65-84.

Dugan, J.P., & Komives, S.R. (2007). *Developing leadership capacity in college students: Findings from a national study.* A Report from the Multi-Institutional Study of Leadership. College Park, MD: National Clearinghouse for Leadership Programs.

Evans, J. N., Forney, D. S., & Guido-DiBrito, F. (1998). *Student development in college: Theory, research, and practice.* San Francisco: Jossey-Bass.

Farber S. (2009). *Greater thank yourself: The ultimate lesson of true leadership.* New York, NY. Doubleday.

Foster, R. (2002). Evaluating outcomes and impacts: A scan of 55 leadership development programs. *W.K. Kellogg Foundation.* (ERIC Document Reproduction)

George, B. (2003). *Authentic leadership: Rediscovering the secrets to creating lasting value.* San Francisco: Jossey-Bass.

Greenleaf, R.K. (2008). *The servant as leader.* Indiana: The Greenleaf Center for Servant Leadership.

Guthre, K.L., Osteen, L. (2012). *Developing students' leadership capacity.* San Francisco: Jossey-Bass.

Hannum, M.K., Martineau, W.J., & Reinelt, C. (2007). *The handbook of leadership development evaluation.* San Francisco: Jossey-Bass.

Higher Education Research Institute (1996). *A social change model of leadership development.* Los Angeles: University of California.

Komives, R. S., Lucas, N., & McMahon, R. T. (1998). *Exploring leadership: For college students who want to make a difference.* San Francisco: Jossey-Bass.

Komives, R.S., Dugan, J.P., Owen, J. E., Slack, C., Wagner, W. (2011). *The handbook for student leadership development.* San Francisco: Jossey-Bass.

Komives, R.S., Longerbeam, D.S., Owen, E.J. Mainella, C.F., Osteen, L. (2006). A leadership identity development model: Applications from a grounded theory. *Journal of College Student Development, 47*(4), 401-418.

Kormanski, C. (1999). *The team: Exploration in group process.* Denver, CO: Love.

Kouzes, J.M., & Posner, B. Z. (2012). *The Leadership Challenge: How to make extraordinary things happen in organizations.* San Francisco: A Wiley Brand.

Lussier, N. R., & Achua, F. C. (2001). *Leadership: Theory, application, and skill development.* Cincinnati, OH: South-Western College.

Marshall, C., & Rossman, G. B. (1999). *Designing qualitative research.* Thousand Oaks, CA: Sage.

Martin, Andrew (2007). *The changing nature of leadership.* The Center for Creative Leadership.

Maxwell, C. J. (1999). *The 21 indispensable qualities of a leader: Becoming the person others will want to follow.* Nashville, TN: Maxwell Motivation.

McMillan, J. H., & Schumacher, S. (2001). *Research in education: A conceptual introduction.* New York: Longman.

Myers & Briggs Foundation. Retrieved May 14, 2014, from http://www.myersbriggs.org

Myers, I. B., & Myers, P. B. (1980). *Gifts differing: Understanding personality type.* Mountain View, CA: Davies-Black.

Northouse, G. P. (2004). *Leadership: Theory and practice.* Thousand Oaks, CA: Sage.

Osteen, L. & Coburn, B.M. (2012). Considering context: Developing students' leadership capacity. *New Directions for Student Services.* (140), 5-15.

Owen, E.J. (2012). Using student development theories as conceptual frameworks in leadership education. *New Directions for Student Services.* (140), 17-35.

Parkinson, H. C. (2004). *Determining the effectiveness of the emerging leader leadership programs offered by Bryant College.* Unpublished manuscript, Nova Southeastern University, Fort Lauderdale, FL.

Roberts, D., & Ullom, C. (1989). Student leadership program model. *NASPA Journal, 27,* 67-74.

Seemiller, C. (2014). *The student leadership competencies guidebook: Designing intentional leadership learning and development.* San Francisco: Jossey-Bass.

Seidman, I. E. (1991). *Interviewing as qualitative research: A guide for researcher in education and the social sciences.* New York: Teachers College Press.

Shankman, M. L. & Allen, S. J. (2008). *Emotionally intelligent leadership: A guide for college students.* San Francisco: Jossey-Bass.

University of Buffalo Leadership Development Center. (2003). *Leadership Development Center programs.* Retrieved October 20, 2003, from www.leadership.buffalo.edu/programs.shtml

Upcraft, M. L., & Schuh, J. H. (1996). *Assessment in student affairs: A guide for practitioners*. San Francisco: Jossey-Bass.

Van Linden, A. J., & Fertman, I. C. (1998). *Youth leadership: A guide to understanding leadership development in adolescents*. San Francisco: Jossey-Bass.

Varcoe, E. K. (2000). *Evaluation methodology learning activity package*. Fort Lauderdale, FL: Nova Southeastern University.

Woodward, B. D., Love, P., & Komives, R. S. (2000). Leadership and management issues for a new century. *New Directions for Student Services, 92*, 5-107.

Woolfolk, A. E. (1998). *Educational psychology*. Boston: Allyn & Bacon.

Zimmerman-Oster, K., & Burkhardt, J. C. (2000). *Leadership in the making: Impact and insights form leadership development programs in U.S. colleges and universities*. Battle Creek, MI: W. K. Kellogg Foundation. (ERIC Document Reproduction Service No. ED446577)

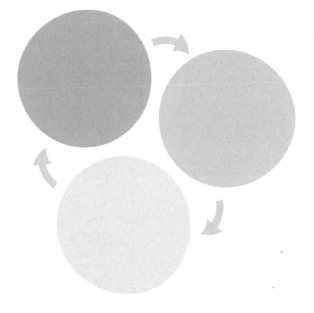